Matters Of The Heart

Keeping the faith

AF520655

notionpress.com

Matters Of The Heart

Keeping the faith

Ratna Magotra

notionpress.com

Notion Press

5 Muthu Kalathy Street, Triplicane,

Chennai - 600 005

First Published by Notion Press 2014

ISBN: 978-93-84049-12-6

This book is dedicated to

All my patients and their courageous families

Acknowledgements

I am deeply grateful to all those who have helped me to put this book together.

First of all, to all the patients and their families who are part of this book.

To all patients who have contributed to my education, training and experience as a general surgeon and then as a cardiothoracic surgeon.

To my teachers and consultants who taught me to stand up with courage and conviction for the rights of the patients.

To all my colleagues, residents, nurses, perfusionists and other staff; without their assistance and help I would not have been able to do anything.

To Aruna Patwardhan, who diligently typed the first draft of the stories as I wrote these in long hand.

I thank friends and well wishers who read these stories and shared their inputs and the criticism. I am especially indebted to Shri N.B Patil for his continuous encouragement to bring out these stories from the old card-board box and prodded me for publishing the same. He translated a few in Marathi and these read better than what I have written.

I thank my family for leaving me with my patients and for their love and affection in allowing me to do things in my way.

I am grateful to Notion Press not only for providing a platform for publishing but also for the patience shown even as I changed and edited the draft of the book several times.

And finally I am most grateful to my friend and philosopher, Krishna, for holding my hand and guiding me along many slippery situations.

Why this book?

My medical career involved practice in highly specialized field of cardio-thoracic surgery in large teaching hospitals in Mumbai. I had made up my mind early to specialize in surgery. Somewhere along the line, I got interested in cardiac surgery. Surgery as a specialty and cardiac surgery in particular were dominated by men. These very men taught me to accept no concessions in the demanding and very competitive specialty for being a woman and give none.

I was generally happy to be where I was, amidst hordes of patients in a public hospital where their endurance and our facilities were always on test.

Amidst buzz of technology and commercialized medical practice, it is easy to miss the 'patient' in the exciting wonders of modern medicine. It is even easier to miss the deep connection between disease and poverty. Heart disease becomes just a little more difficult when patient is a young woman especially from rural area, once she gets stigmatized with heart disease. Economic burden caused to the family is immense and ordeal does not stop with only medical or surgical treatment.

The patients came from diverse social and cultural backgrounds but shared their poverty besides their heart disease. It was amazing how this common bond held them together in the most hostile environment. Those familiar with the impersonal and unfriendly public hospitals will know what I mean.

During my interactions with patients and families, they were gracious to let me peep in their lives. I started looking beyond the obvious and reflect beyond the operation theatre. The idea of putting some of these experiences on paper had been with me for a long time. In fact most of these were written before I left K E M hospital in the year 2000.

Some patients left a very deep impression because of their poise and immense inner strength in the face of adversity.

And lastly this book is result of keen desire to demystify the heart surgery. Operation theatre is an arena for great drama and is appropriately named so. Open heart surgery can be called mother of all drama. Patients and public at large do not generally know what goes on inside even as they repose great trust in their doctors. Most people associate heart surgery with bypass, angioplasty and stents. Heart disease other than coronary artery disease is full of intrigue and complexity like that for birth defects or rheumatic heart disease affecting the delicate heart valves. Some of these operations are far more intricate and challenging when compared to 'bypass'. An attempt has been made to describe open heart operations in simple language. This was a long standing request from patients and their families, few of whom are part of this book.

These stories were written long back and events relate to even earlier times. Technology has extended the reach and safety of cardiac surgery since then. New paradigms have emerged especially in congenital heart surgery where very young infants including newborns are being routinely operated upon successfully at many centers in India.

With advances in fetal medicine, there is an argument for terminating pregnancies with serious anomalies. There was much debate couple of years back when a Mumbai couple (Nikita Mehta case) approached the courts to amend the law for medical termination after they found out the baby to have congenital heart problem. The readers are free to make their choices and conclusions.

Ratna Magotra

Contents

WHITE BOAT WITH A BLUE SAIL

Every surgeon has experienced situations through his or her professional career for which there are no logical explanations. A seemingly simple operation can occasionally result in a dismal outcome while another more complicated and complex procedure meets with an unexpected but spectacular recovery. When one operates on high risk patients, success brings accolades, elation, pride and rewards to the surgeon. The failure, in such high risk cases, too is accepted both by the surgeon and the family.

However, when simple cases go wrong, it leaves everyone in deep distress and desolation. Sometimes patients have strong premonitions about the outcome that prove right to everyone's surprise.

A death occurring on operation table is indeed most painful experience for any surgeon.

While one can understand the grief of the family and empathize with them, not many perhaps know the pain and anguish it must cause to the surgeon and other members of the team. It is only now after nearly thirty-plus years of working as a surgeon that I can share what goes through the surgeon's mind at times like this. The emotions are more than just a mix of personal failure and an overwhelming guilt.

The surgeon alone is responsible to the family of the unfortunate patient. He or she has to lead the team and as the captain of the team, tends to the expectations of the patients and the morale of the team. It is lonely at the top and there is no one to share one's own emotions and pain with. As one matures beyond the dare devilry of youth and gets wiser to realize that the doctors need not try to become gods. Success and failure both need to be faced with a measure of equanimity.

"Karmanay vaadhikar aste, ma phalesu kadachina"

Priya was niece of my roommate. She also remains the most beautiful child in my memory. When I first saw Priya and looked around the first reaction was that she did not belong here. She had an ethereal look about her. She was four years of age at that time. Her milk and peaches complexion, large green eyes and red lips on a beautifully chiseled face framed in long golden curls had me almost transfixed. Everything about her was poetry in beauty and grace. She was soft and fragile. One almost felt an instant desire to touch her and yet afraid to do so lest the touch left a trace of dirt on her fair skin. She was a quiet child, very calm and serene. I also noticed that she was mostly playing by herself.

It was after some time that I came to know that she had a congenital heart defect, a large hole in the heart. She would get tired easily and had instinctively learnt not to overstretch her limits.

The heart defect could be considered as the only blemish in the otherwise perfect creation of God.

I had only recently started residency in General Surgery and was sharing the room with another resident in Pediatrics. We soon became good friends and spent lot of time together. We often discussed Priya's heart condition. We felt reassured that the modern medicine had reached the sophistication where Priya's simple heart defect could be fixed without much difficulty.

Priya had a fairly large hole in her heart. The heart had enlarged considerably and the increased blood flow through the lungs had elevated the pressure in the pulmonary artery, that carries blood from the right heart to both the lungs for oxygenation. As such the defect was not likely to close on its own and the pulmonary pressure was likely to increase further as the time went by. We were often in the library poring over details related to atrial septal defect (ASD) and were greatly relieved to learn that the ASD was the simplest of all birth defects of the heart requiring open-heart surgery. The risk of the operation was extremely low and after the operation, one could enjoy normal life especially when the operation was performed in early childhood. Though if not operated upon the pulmonary hypertension could become irreversible and blood shunting in reverse making the condition inoperable.

Excited with our freshly minted knowledge we found ourselves keeping close tabs on what was happening in the heart surgery unit in our hospital. The cardiac surgery residents were best known for an air of superiority and treated others coming from general surgery as lowly creatures limited to dealing only with piles, hernias and hydroceles! For once we were ready to ignore their patronizing attitude as we made quiet rounds of patients recuperating after heart surgery. Looking at some of them we soon developed new respect for the cardiac team specially after witnessing a baby with deep blue lips and nails who returned from the O.R. looking bright and pink after a shunt surgery. It was no less than a miracle.

Priya in the meantime was troubled with frequent respiratory infections and was getting tired easily. The pediatrician too advised early operation. The task of convincing the family was left to us, the young medicos. The family especially the mother was apprehensive but finally agreed for the operation in a private hospital. Once the decision was made, we took the lead in making arrangements for the operation.

Priya was admitted in the hospital two days before her operation. The hospital was a very exclusive private clinic, clean and swanky with its white paint and wide corridors; the room had its own balcony overlooking the blue sea. The lily white soft linen on the bed was in sharp contrast with the stained sheets in the wards of our general hospital. Everything in her room was white including the flowers by her bedside. Priya herself was thrilled to be there as she gazed at the blue sea from her room. I had never before seen her looking so happy.

Priya had the usual pre-operative work up. Echo-Cardiography had not yet become available. There were no sophisticated angiography laboratories either. A cardiac catheterization was done on simple radiological machine with cut films in the railway hospital nearby, only place with such facilities.

The evening before the operation, we were in the spacious balcony of her room watching the sea. The sea was quiet and calm. Some large ships were silhouetted at a distance against the setting sun while a few small boats bobbed up and down, swayed by the gentle waves nearby. A white boat with a blue sail caught Priya's fancy and she kept gazing at this boat. We must have stood there for a long time as the dusk progressed into dark night. The tiny lights sparkling and shimmering in the water had replaced the beautiful colors of the sun set. Priya made a surreal sight in this background.

Suddenly Priya spoke in a very calm and soft voice, "Tomorrow I shall go sailing in that white boat". As she refused to leave the place she was reassured with a promise to take her for the boat ride after the operation. Priya's large eyes deep like a lake betrayed no signs of excitement or fear in her eyes about the operation next morning. A quiet smile was playing on her lips and she whispered calmly, "but I will be going tomorrow itself - in that white boat". She pointed her slim finger towards the sea where we had been observing the boats a little while ago, now engulfed in the darkness. The nurse came in and took Priya to the bed closing the balcony door behind her. As she gave Priya a spoonful of chloral hydrate syrup to ensure she slept well. As the nurse adjusted the bed linen, Priya asked the nurse with a twinkle in her eye, "Please sister, can you open the balcony door, I like those lights in the sea". The nurse opened the door a little bit telling us to close the same once Priya went off to sleep. There was a slight nip in the cool December breeze.

We sat there in silence as Priya drifted into chloral hydrate induced sleep clutching the soft white pillow. We were glad that she had made no fuss in the hospital and wondered if she understood that she was there to undergo a major open-heart operation. Priya's mother came soon after. We had lost all appetite and for the first time felt nervous with the enormous responsibility that we had taken upon ourselves. Priya's parents and grandparents had asked us no questions and had left everything to us. I did not sleep much that night and came back early next morning.

When we reached the hospital, Priya was dressed in an oversized green gown looking very pretty and happy. Her mother told us that she had slept well the previous night. Other close relatives too were waiting outside her room. Being a surgical resident, I had the permission of the surgeon to attend the operation while my friend waited outside with rest of the family.

The operation progressed smoothly, though at that stage, I did not quite comprehend much of what was happening. The surgeon had hooked her on the heart lung machine by the time I could manage to have a peep in the operation area. The surgeon, tall and majestic with clear eyes signaled me to move near the head end. Timidly I stepped by the side of the anesthesiologist, almost afraid of touching or disconnecting the plethora of plastic tubes spread all around. The genial and mild mannered anesthetist reassured me as he made space for me to balance on a raised platform stool. I could at last see the area where all action was taking place. The heart had become still and was looking pale. I could hardly associate this sight with Priya and before I could orient my knowledge of the anatomy of the heart, the surgeon was showing me a large gaping hole in the wall separating the right and the left chambers of the heart. He turned to the scrub nurse as he asked her for the 'Dacron patch'. The nurse removed the surgical patch after peeling open a sterile pack and handed over to the surgeon. The surgeon fashioned the patch into an oval strip, little larger than the size of the hole in the heart and sewed it deftly with special sutures, covering the gaping hole. He was already closing the right chamber of the heart, when he asked the technician to re-warm the patient and also asked him to run a blood sample for gas and potassium report. It had not taken more than 15 minutes to finish the job inside the heart and as the surgeon released the cross clamp from the aorta, the heart had started fibrillating. The nurse adjusted tiny defibrillator paddles and passed the long cord over the surgical drapes to the anesthetist, who connected it to a black colored machine, called defibrillator. He now asked me to step aside as the operation was over and he needed the space. The surgeon asked everybody to step away from the table as the anesthetist pressed the black button on the machine. As the current passed through the heart, I felt sick, almost entire body of Priya had arched and the heart was nearly out of the chest. I tried to steady myself as the heart started to beat feebly before it fibrillated again. Another shock and the same sequence followed again. As the heart just refused to beat after repeated shocks, the technician was asked to go back on full bypass and run another gas and potassium test. By this time, few beads of sweat had appeared on the surgeon's forehead although the O.R was chilled and his movements had betrayed no signs of nervousness. A circulating nurse stepped ahead and wiped the surgeon's brow with a gauze piece. Blood gas and potassium reports were normal and the surgeon proceeded to deliver another shock with increased current. This time the heart started to beat and a sigh of relief escaped from the lips of practically everyone present in the room. It had been nearly an hour since the cross clamp had been removed. Everything looked all right for next fifteen minutes or so. But as the surgeon prepared to disconnect the heart lung machine, the heart beat stopped. This time, all activity had ceased. There was no fibrillation, not even gentle quivering. The heart had started to dilate and the surgeon ordered the technician to go back on bypass, his voice still cool and poised. My mouth, however, was dry, my lips parched and the legs were giving way. I withdrew myself into a corner from where I could not see several unsuccessful attempts that were made to revive the heart during next couple of hours. The feelings of guilt had overpowered me and I was blaming myself for pushing Priya to her end. We could have waited for some more time – or suppose we had not operated at all – I was torn with several emotions as I dragged myself, petrified to break the news to my friend and her relatives. I felt relieved to see that the surgeon was already there and had explained, as best as he could, the tragic circumstances to the family members. They were shocked and devastated yet a picture of dignity in accepting this as God's will.

The events after that were mechanical though I found it difficult to face the family. I offered to stay back and take care of the formalities. As the death had occurred in the O.R police formalities and Coroner's clearance were necessary before Priya's frail body could be taken home for the funeral rites and the final journey.

While the paper work was being completed, I went to her room with a heavy heart to pick up her personal effects. It was nearly evening; the entire day had passed without any sense of time. The anticipation of successful outcome had been replaced with gloom and sadness. Once in her room, I stood silent and motionless completely drained with no strength to pick up her little things including her favorite doll that she had insisted on bringing along. It was difficult to accept that Priya's operation had gone horribly wrong and that she was no more with us.

The mind turned to the previous evening and my eyes turned towards the balcony. The door was half open. I was looking at the sea through teary eyes. The sea that was looking so inviting, bright and gay last night was now sad and quiet. I also noticed that the white boat with blue sail had gone.

WHAT IS IN A NAME

One born of natural parents grows up with kin, broadly known as relatives. Some other relations are nurtured as one grows forging new dimensions of friendship, one gets married and has children. One's last name is identified with family surname in most cultures and ethnic backgrounds.

For several years between 1961 and 1974, Arvindbhai was an integral member of the staff in experimental surgery laboratory until Dr. Dastur retired. Ho took no salary but worked longer hours than anyone else did. First time I saw Arvindbhai in the experimental laboratory, I mistook him for a senior research officer. I was not the only one to do so as many newcomers in the department had had the same impression before me. He was always dressed in white trousers and a white bush-shirt, top two buttons of which were left carelessly open. A thick gold chain could be seen caressing a thick brownish scar with ugly zigzag margins running through the exposed mid-chest running from almost his short neck downwards. Arvindbhai never looked embarrassed by this ugly scar. His position amongst the staff defied any description. He always found a ready and eager audience amongst the fresh recruits and one lazy afternoon Arvindbhai told us how he had landed in

Dr. Dastur's laboratory. We were surprised that he had no medical training of any type; in fact he was working as a news correspondent before joining the honorary roll in the experimental laboratory. Between these two jobs was a tale of great interest, suffering and high emotions.

Arvind-Dastur-Lillehei, as he introduced himself, was indeed a strange and unusual name. Orphaned and abandoned at a very young age, he was known only by his first name, Arvind, for the first twenty two odd years of his life. He had a pretty lonely life bereft of any close relationship with anyone. He was born in a small village in Saurashtra in Gujarat. He was not two years old when both parents died in some epidemic that he called plague –like disease. His maternal uncle brought him home but his aunt never really liked the idea of having one more mouth to feed. As the aunt's irritation grew, so did his rude behavior towards her. This mutual dislike was giving him sadistic pleasure. Matters came to a head with no chance of settlement even as his mild mannered uncle tried his best to make the troubled relationship work to the minimum civil behavior. It became difficult for the uncle also to defend his sassy nature. Arvind thus drifted away from the only person who had provided him some affection and care. He started spending more and more time away from home with the village lads who themselves were mostly school drop-outs. His future was as hazy as the winter fog. Arvind clever as he was soon became disenchanted with the rudderless life and started looking for opportunities to go to the city. He left his uncle's home one night never to return. His only regret being going away from the uncle, the only affection that he had ever experienced. He eventually landed on the streets of Bombay (now Mumbai). He was only ten or eleven at the time but was sharp with tongue and intelligent. Streets of Bombay welcomed him. He shared the footpath with Ganu, Laxmi, Bapu and others. They were a happy lot; none probed the past of the other and they lived for the day without a care. He soon found a shelter near Grant Road station and joined boys of his age polishing shoes outside the railway station though he did not like it much. Next he started distributing morning newspapers and milk bottles came next as the agent was happy with his work. This gave him chance to befriend families by making small talk. He was not lazy and rain or shine, Arvind was dependable to bring the goods on time and without a break. Arvind liked his new found importance as first time somebody was waiting for him or missing him if he did not show up. A gentle compassionate Parsi lady allowed him to sleep in her verandah during famous monsoons of Bombay. She never asked him to leave even after the rains were over. Arvind was grateful as he now had a place he could call home to return to after he was done with the daily errands.

A friendship grew between Mrs. Veluporia and Arvind; he would help her with groceries or running to the post office and doing odd jobs for her. She told him that she was living alone since her husband died a few years back and both her children were abroad. She herself came from an affluent family and was involved with some charitable organizations. She permitted

Arvind to do more household chores with a condition that he enrolled in a night school. Arvind grabbed the only chance to turn a leaf in his life. It was during this time when he must have been about 13 or 14 that he developed high fever and had joint pains making it difficult for him to move around. Mrs. Veluporia looked after him like he was her own child and took him to the doctor. He soon recovered and was back to his old self. A glass of Ovaltine at night continued from Mrs. Veluporia for several weeks even after he had fully recovered.

Arvind passed the High school examination with average pass marks but Mrs. Veluporia was delighted. Arvind started to look for a regular job though the gentle lady would not mind supporting him through college. It was the saddest day for Arvind when Mrs. Veluporia passed away. Arvind was inconsolable and he sobbed like a baby. He had no clear memory of his own parents and she was closest to anyone he would know as a mother. He grieved for the old lady and felt he had been orphaned all over again. After some days, her son came from America to wind up and left soon after. Arvind had once again lost his home.

He was back on the streets but this time not for long. He soon found a job in a newspaper office that would allow him to sleep there at night. Once he settled down in his new abode, his curious nature made him look around the day's remnants, papers, news items corrected, scrapped and tossed away. It became a good time pass for him to go through many of such papers lying around as he got the place ready for the next day. He also discovered to his own surprise that he really had a nose for collecting news. He could make friends even with strangers and that came handy in garnering the local gossip. Stories came easily to him. This impressed the small time editor of the paper and he was assigned the beat as a junior correspondent. He was not exactly independent which he would have liked to be, he had to report to an elderly sub-editor who would then build the gossip into an interesting item. Arvind was excited to see his name in print once the sub-editor started to give him the by-line. Soon he was covering the local events and filing reports. His circle of friends also grew with newfound status. On his part, Arvind never liked serious news, his own life had been too painful and traumatic and he had no desire to visit death and gore that was becoming serious news. Both he and his newspaper lacked the depth and analytic power and were happy to cater to locals. Arvind missed Mrs. Veluporia but was happy with the way things had happened after her demise. As his running around increased, Arvind became conscious that he was getting tired easily and sometimes experienced shortness of breath. He realized that he had to stop several times if he was trying to run to catch a train or bus or even when he had to climb a flight of stairs to meet someone.

Dr. Dastur's clinic was on the first floor of the same building where Arvind's office was located. He had passed the doctor on many occasions but had not got much beyond a nod or sometimes a faint hint of a smile. Arvind had liked the doctor and as was his nature he would have preferred to know little more about him. He found it difficult to break the ice with this reserved doctor. He heard from others that Dr. Dastur was a very eminent surgeon in a city hospital with a flourishing private practice. Arvind took his recent symptoms as the perfect opportunity to approach the doctor and strike the right chord to befriend him. The doctor would surely not refuse a newspaper man.

He was admitted to the doctor's office without any fuss. To his utter surprise he found himself tongue-tied as he found himself sat facing the man he was trying hard to befriend. Dr. Dastur listened patiently before waiving him to move to the examination couch. Arvind noticed doctor's expression becoming serious as Arvind got dressed and tried to become a little chirpy. Doctor meanwhile was looking intently at his face as Arvind nervously settled back in the chair facing the doctor. Doctor very politely asked him if he had come alone or any family member was waiting outside. Arvind then told the doctor that he lived alone and as such had no family. The doctor was silent for some time before breaking the news to him that he suspected him to have heart disease affecting one of the heart valves. He prescribed him some tablets and gave a note referring him to Nair hospital for further tests before he could confirm the diagnosis. Doctor's words were spoken softly yet had the effect of a brick house falling on his head. Heart disease was not even in his thoughts when he had walked in a little while ago. As he dragged himself to his office, several thoughts were flashing by, how he could have heart disease... what does a leaking valve has to do with the heart; he didn't even know that heart has some valves inside. Only thing he knew at that time was that heart disease was the last thing he could afford to have at this stage of his life. All thoughts about interviewing the doctor or filing an article on him had vanished from his mind.

He was worried like hell and felt exhausted as he sank in his low bed.

He set the fan at its maximum speed as he felt himself choking even as his heart raced at a faster rate. He sipped a little water. He could not allow the fear to take over his life. He thought to himself that he could not die so young without fulfiling his dream of doing something "worthwhile' whatever that meant. He decided to follow the advice and go for further tests. He felt better with the medicines and soon he was his earlier self joking, laughing and making merry and got busy with gathering news as before.

He did go to the Nair hospital, more to make friends with Dr. Dastur. He had really liked this doctor and wished to know more about him. If he had to go to the hospital and undergo some tests, so be it he suggested to himself.

He was asked to take an X-Ray of the chest and then go to another room for an electric recording of the heart where the machine stopped half way after making some spluttering noises. While other patients grumbled, it was quite alright with Arvind, who came back on another day. As he waited to see Dr. Dastur with the reports, he had done some research on the doctor befriending some hospital staff and getting into casual conversations with them. He learnt that though Dastur looked very unassuming, he was a pioneer in open heart surgery in India. Just a year back he had performed an operation to close a hole in the heart of a young girl and that too with a machine that the doctor had designed and got manufactured in Bombay itself. This was when all most all equipment being used in the hospitals was imported and very expensive. This was a coup of a sort for Arvind. His admiration and respect for the doctor grew several folds and he thought he had a story to tell through his newspaper.

He started to visit Nair hospital more often and found himself in the experimental surgery laboratory, popularly called as dog-lab where Dr. Dastur spent lot of time trying to perfect techniques of open heart surgery. He soon learnt that Dr. Dastur and his team were operating on dogs whenever they were not operating on human beings in the hospital. These were very early days and only simple operations were being carried out on the patients. More meat to the story, Arvind had rehashed many stories on Dr. Dastur but only in his mind. He had not put even a line on the paper.

Arvind soon found himself spending more time in the dog-lab doing odd jobs; he had become Man Friday for Dr. Dastur, keeping notes, filing reports, getting requisite permissions from the authorities concerned whenever and wherever required, so on and so forth. At times he was an electrician fixing some broken switches or wires and if the cleaner didn't show up on some day, Arvind would happily sweep the messy floor of the dog lab. He soon realized that early sixties were heady days of cardiac surgery as new breakthroughs were happening across the world practically every day. Dr. Dastur would reach the lab excitedly and in a hurry to do something new whenever he had read or had come to know about something new happening in the United States or Europe. Dastur and his team were working feverishly trying new techniques, new drugs to stop the heart or tweak heart-lung machine to give better results. Arvind became part of this exciting process as he spent more time in the laboratory than in his office. His absence from the office meanwhile had not gone unnoticed by his employers. The regular staff of the hospital on the other hand was only happy with his help as they felt over worked with this extra work after regular hours in the hospital with the patients. Some of the house staff didn't really like to work in the dog laboratory though they had very little option to say no to an exacting chief. Arvind would gladly cover for such residents. He would eavesdrop on names like Lillehei and Cooley while Dr. Dastur would be discussing with colleagues; one fine day he overheard them discussing that a successful operation replacing heart valve had taken place in the United States. Open heart surgery prior to this was being done mainly for birth defects called congenital heart disease in medical parlance. Arvind was up in excitement and asked if Dr. Dastur was ready to change his leaking valve. Dr. Dastur only smiled in return.

Arvind was gradually getting more breathless despite taking the medicines regularly. He had almost stopped his regular beat as a news person since that required fair amount of running around in public transport. Working in the laboratory helped him to adapt to his worsening heart condition. He received no salary from the hospital and if Dr. Dastur was paying him something on his own nobody knew about it. He now spent most of his time with Dr. Dastur, in his clinic and hospitals when not in the laboratory. No one, therefore, was surprised when he started calling himself Arvind Dastur from just Arvind.

He would ask Dr. Dastur every now and then if he (Dastur) would operate on him to change the defective heart valve. Those days there were no artificial heart valves available in India, attempts at repairing the heart valves were unsuccessful and not really encouraging clinically in human patients; as a matter of fact heart valve surgery using artificial valves was in its infancy even in the developed countries. Dr. Dastur would gently explain to him that though the doctors here could do the surgery, they need to have the mechanical heart valves in their armamentarium. The surgeons also knew that the foreign exchange regulations and strict import policies would not allow them this luxury very near in the future.

The days ticked by and routine chores continued for Arvind until one day he saw Dr. Dastur making quick strides into the hospital and looking very excited. As soon as all collected around his table as was the custom, Dr. Dastur took out a long list from his pocket and started to assign different tasks to each one. Dr. C Walton Lillehei from University of Minnesota, USA was arriving in Bombay (now Mumbai) and he was scheduled to visit the "dog-lab" of Dastur. Arvind was asked to get the laboratory in order, the records neatly laid out, the animal house cleaned and if possible to get an experiment going when the famous heart surgeon came visiting the hospital. Once Dr. Dastur left, the hushed silence converted into murmurs and then almost a din of excitement of Dr. Lillehei visiting Nair hospital. Arvind learnt during the charged discussions about Lillehei that he was the real pioneer in open heart surgery. His earlier feats involved in correcting several congenital heart defects by innovative technique of 'controlled cross circulation' where a parent was used, connected as a temporary oxygenator for repairing the heart defects by open heart surgery. He was already a legend and surgeons everywhere were excited with new possibilities in open heart surgery arena. The big day was nearing. Arvind got the entire laboratory cleaned and scrubbed, the dogs were not spared either. Victor, the first survivor (amongst dogs) of Dastur's heart lung machine experiments was to be showcased as a hero.

Lillehei arrived accompanied by his team and proceeded immediately to make rounds in the surgical wards where he met couple of patients recovering after open heart surgery. He was keen to visit the laboratory and Dr. Dastur too wanted the lab visit as highlight of open heart surgery program at the hospital. Lillehei was impressed that first open heart surgery was done with a locally developed heart-lung machine. He complimented Dr. Dastur for wonderful work with the dog experiments. Once in the lab Dr. Dastur proudly introduced the team members to Lillehei as they finished presenting the data on the experiments each one was involved with. Lillehei was generous with the praise for the work being done with limited resources available to Dr. Dastur. Arvind had caught Lillehei's eye as he saw him scurrying about but had not been formally introduced to him so far. They were seated for lunch when Dr. Dastur mentioned about Arvind whom he called a 'patient-researcher'. He told Lillehei that Arvind had a severely leaking mitral valve that needed surgery and how they were constrained since no artificial heart valves were as yet available to him. He didn't forget to mention how keen Arvind was to get operated upon and his involvement in experimental heart surgery at the Nair hospital without any degree, qualification or remuneration! Arvind too was contributing to development of heart surgery in the hospital. Since Arvind was not burdened by any official definition of his job, he had the freedom to do what pleased him from scrubbing the animals to helping in experiments and even disposing off the unfortunate dogs that died during the experiments. Lillehei did not forget to appreciate Arvind and while leaving patted him lightly on the shoulder and asked him if he would like to come to the United Sates for his heart valve operation. Arvind did not understand much though prompted by Dr. Dastur, he murmured words of gratitude for the offer and got busy settling the mess as everyone promptly left as the procession disappeared.

More than Arvind, it was Dr. Dastur who was taken aback on receiving a letter from Lillehei after a few weeks; Lillehei had high praise for the work being done at the Nair hospital and had added that Arvind could come to Minnesota for his heart valve surgery and that too free of cost. Lillehei explained in details about a new heart valve he had designed in his research laboratory and was enrolling new patients in whom this valve could be used. It was clear that the valve was being investigated though Lillehei was sure that this would work. Since Arvind was so motivated for his heart operation, he would be an ideal patient. Arvind didn't take longer than a moment to express his willingness to travel to U.S for the operation. Dastur arranged for his ticket and visa formalities; he also had to sign, in the capacity of legal guardian, the elaborate consent forms and other documents that

Lillehei sent once he was informed that Arvind was ready to volunteer for heart valve replacement using Lillehei's new valve.

Arvind flew into Minnesota on a cold morning and was received by a hospital nurse. He was admitted to the hospital straightaway. The hospital environment was very different from what Arvind was used to in India. If this intimidated Arvind, he was too excited to betray any emotions of fear or anxiety. As was his nature he made friends with the doctors, nurses and patients. He found American people very friendly. He was delighted to see Lillehei on rounds after a couple of days and was pleased as punch when he greeted him by his name. Lillehei didn't forget to tell his associates about Arvind's incredible dedication to experimental cardiac surgery laboratory in Bombay.

He underwent several tests while in the hospital. He was made to go through a pile of documents as the nurse explained that the heart valve was new and still under investigations and there was no long term survivors as such. She also explained broadly how Lillehei would carry out the operation and likely post-operative recovery in the intensive care where he would find himself hooked up to various gadgets once he woke up after the operation. She probably left unsaid if he woke up! Arvind was operated upon and his grossly damaged heart valve was replaced with the new metallic heart valve prosthesis. To everyone's surprise Arvind's recovery was phenomenally fast. Lillehei was very pleased and had already informed Dastur on phone about the successful operation. Arvind's popularity soared after the operation as he became a mini celebrity in the post-operative ward. Several doctors and even the visitors arrived to see him and everyone greeted him warmly. Teams of various doctors were carrying out elaborate tests on him. Arvind was flattered as a nurse was in charge solely for him and she kept elaborate records of his recovery and various tests being done on him. He himself was very impressed the way records were maintained and made several notes himself for implementing some of this on his return.

Arvind could hear the new valve loud and clear in his chest with every heart beat. Though the noise was quite loud, Arvind was not complaining. He was happy that he had become a part of an important event in heart surgery and that too in America. He sometimes felt a twinge of sadness that he could not be operated upon by his doctor, Dastur at the Nair hospital.

There was a setback in his recovery when he started running fever few days after surgery and this was diagnosed to be because of pneumonia. There was tremendous anxiety amongst the doctors and nurses looking after him as the infection could settle on the new heart valve. That would be a serious complication and ruin the result of otherwise successful heart valve surgery. Arvind recovered fast to everyone's relief and had no further problems till the time of his discharge from the hospital. Returning to India was still far as he had to stay back for necessary follow-up and collection of further data on the valve. A small apartment had been arranged by the hospital where he would stay without his having to pay for any thing. He had been started on blood thinners for which he required frequent blood tests to adjust the best dosage of the medication. If it was too much, he could have a fatal bleed and if too little, there was possibility of a clot sitting on the valve. Further this clot would not only hamper the valve function but some fragments could become loose and even go to his brain resulting in a stroke. All this had been explained to him before the operation too though now it was reinforced by the nurse on every visit.

Once in the apartment alone except brief contact with others during his visit to the clinic or cafeteria, Arvind started missing home or to be more precise Nair hospital. He was longing to come home and share this life changing experience with Dastur and other staff. It was nearly five months in the US when finally he was allowed to leave for India. Lillehei and his team of researchers were extremely happy with the data they had got on the heart valve. The nurses had arranged a farewell party for their dear patient where Lillehei also made a brief appearance. Arvind fought the tears as he had never ever received this sort of attention or affection. He thanked all as best as he could manage with his English becoming a casualty of his emotions.

Once aboard the plane, he was elated and yet with mixed emotions he had started missing the hospital and people he was leaving behind.

Overwhelmed on landing in Bombay, he took a deep breath of familiar hot and humid air and liked the experience and he inhaled again this time more deeply than before. The Indian air, elixir of life, was merging with the life sustaining sounds of foreign heart valve opening and closing with every heart beat.

As Arvind made his way out of the winding immigration formalities, he saw through eyes welled with tears that Dr. Dastur with a few members of staff were there to receive their favorite 'researcher-patient' now a celebrity- Arvind-Dastur-Lillehei.

ANGELS IN THE OUTFIELD

Normally the human child has 46 chromosomes, 23 inherited from each parent. These chromosomes contain the genetic information. In Down's syndrome also called Trisomy 21, there is an extra chromosome (21) that results in typical facial features also referred to as Mongoloid features. The face is usually rounded with slanting eyes with prominent inner (epicanthal) fold, tongue may be thick and protruding in some children. They may have shorter limbs with flat palms, reduced muscle tone and developmental milestones may be delayed. These children suffer from frequent infections, digestive problems and may have congenital heart defects. The mental capabilities vary from mild impairment to serious retardation. Average IQ of these children is reported to be around 50. Many children with Down Syndrome need intense family support, special enrichment therapies though a few children can grow to a gainful education and employment. There are moral and ethical issues related to these children depending upon severity of the associated problems.

The World Down Syndrome Day was held on 21 March 2006. The day and month were chosen to correspond with 21 and trisomy respectively and has been recognized by WHO.

Mary Kutty glanced through the draft of her speech. She was to speak at a function to celebrate a decade of service by "Foundation of Rehabilitation of Down's children" (FORD), an organization founded by Mary herself. She dressed up quickly without betraying any nervousness as she left along with daughter Tracy to pick up her husband Varghese from the office and headed for the venue. Varghese had made it a habit to accompany Mary for most of her talks and felt a personal pride to see a very consummate Mary talking her way to medical experts and the lay persons with great aplomb. On this occasion he noticed that Mary was quiet on the way; he thought this as natural for she was to reflect upon ten years of hard work by her and her foundation in giving a direction to these special children. On reaching the venue, Mary nodded approvingly to her staff as the hall was tastefully decorated, the parents and children from her foundation were seated in rows reserved for them while the professionals and guests filled rest of the auditorium. She could spot a few doctors working in special clinics of children. The press enclosure was also well occupied. Verghese and Tracy headed towards their seats as Mary was welcomed and escorted towards the dais. The children dressed in their best and her daughter, sitting amongst the audience, gave a broad smile to Mary. She had regained her composure and confidence. She folded her prepared speech neatly and put it in her handbag. She did not need any written notes to talk about her life's work.

She spoke slowly to begin with emphasizing the milestones of the organization. She then continued in an animated voice, "their simplicity and slow mental abilities are hurdles only for themselves and they are no threat to the society. These children are devoid of any 'greed' or destructive traits of aggression seen and even encouraged in many normal children in the society. Not only these children are happy and contended, they also bring out the best qualities in those looking after them. Then why some people are advocating that life could be snuffed out even before they are born? The experts claim to voice their opinion out of concern for these children. I suspect that they consider these children as social burden, on the parents and the society! These children are not merely technical or scientific issues, they are real. So many 'normal' individuals in the modern society have social deviations and perversions - psychologists and human right experts exhort the society to take a lenient view of their delinquencies. Aggression or killing spirit is considered necessary quality in the survival kit of today's young people. Then why are these harmless children with Down's syndrome considered a threat to the society and the experts advocate that the mothers exercise their choice to abort these children? Should medical experts treat every problem of human body in a mechanistic manner - what cannot be fixed should be discarded or replaced? The violence prevalent in the otherwise civil societies cannot always be attributed to genetic profile of individuals; at least some results from a cultural and structural void brought about by emphasis on too much perfection in physical, mental and emotional being of the individuals. The culture of affluence and craze for perfection has pervaded the micro levels of the social organization whereas love and compassion should be the real values as professed by Jesus. Our doctors make and justify their heroic efforts in the intensive care units where terminally ill and ageing people are kept on costly intensive life support systems for prolonged periods. They know it well that they cannot ward off death permanently but only postpone it by a few hours, few days or may be few months. How can few experts, far removed from caring of actual people sitting in their ivory towers in a university or a television studio decide about quality of life or about human happiness? These experts pose as neutral experts but in fact carry overtones of personal prejudices and biases. The healthy individuals can take health for granted and smug with their own physical and genetic well being find it difficult to accept any lesser being. Every child has a certain worth to the family and can teach lessons of compassion to the parents, siblings, friends and indeed the entire society."

Mary paused briefly as her eyes panned across the hall. Verghese shuffled in his chair. He had never heard Mary speak with such passion. She had relived her own life and that of the organization. Mary and the entire audience were in almost a spiritual communication. What they didn't know was that the angst of Mary originated a few days back when she was listening to a TV debate on rights of a woman for choice to abort a fetus with complex heart defects. As she continued her speech, she was not speaking the words in anger anymore, "ethics and morals are variable and often contradictory when one talks of childbirth or reproduction and choices related to these. Some might consider it unethical to allow a child to be born only to lead a helpless, dependant life with severe limitations of physical and emotional health especially when technology is available to diagnose severe abnormalities very early in pregnancy. Future of these children actually should unite all on either side of the divide. Those who go against the medical advice need not feel guilty for producing a child who is not perfect but it is incumbent that they and the society take full responsibility for their future needs. Fortunately science and advances in medical technology also bring a lot of hope. There will be technology in future for selectively treating these genes even in the unborn children that may allow these babies to grow normal, both physically and mentally. Until such time, special efforts need to be directed at their rehabilitation and education to give them a full and rich life. The technology today can pool the best efforts and newer therapies in form of art, music, animation and wide range of software could be harnessed in an effective manner. The future efforts should be directed at assimilation of these children and adolescents within the normal communities instead of isolating them. Their limitations will in no way limit the potentials of normal children but can only enhance their finer inner qualities".

Mary finished her speech to a thunderous applause but the claps that cheered her most were from soft and chubby hands, coming from the special enclosure where children with Down's syndrome were sitting like little angels in the outfield. Tracy, her daughter was one of them.

Tracy was diagnosed to be a Down's syndrome baby when she was 4 months of age. The diagnosis had shocked Mary. She spent long hours in the clinics of different specialists hoping in vain that the next specialist might set the diagnosis right made perhaps erroneously by the previous doctor of Tracy being a Down's baby. The genetic clinic at the medical college hospital at last put all her doubts at rest. All the tests carried out there confirmed that Tracy carried an extra chromosome on her gene 21 and was indeed a case of Down's syndrome. Children affected by this chromosomal abnormality were also called Mongoloids because of their typical features, deeply set and slanted eyes with prominent inner folds! These children were slow learners, could be physically and mentally challenged and very often unable to take care of themselves. Mary sank in despair as the doctors unfolded the mysteries of Down's syndrome before her and her husband, Verghese. Their pain was further compounded with a terrible sense of guilt when they were told that elderly couples like them were more likely to have babies affected with such chromosomal abnormalities. Mary and Verghese felt their happy dreams crashing in front of their eyes. They had considered themselves extremely fortunate and blessed when Tracy was born two years after their dream marriage.

Mary was working as an executive secretary in a private firm and Verghese had a small business of his own. He used to visit Mary's office often in connection with his business deals. Both of them, alone in the city, struck a beautiful friendship culminating into marriage after a brief courtship. Mary came from a conservative family living in Kerala and was working for a private company in Bombay (now Mumbai). The proprietor of the company was a distant cousin of her mother and when his business expanded and he moved his company to Bombay, he requested Mary's mother to send her daughter for taking care of his new office. Both she and her mother readily agreed to the proposal. He had always helped them in their hour of need and when he needed somebody reliable to look after his office in a new place, this could be one way of repaying the debt. Mary had abundant qualities of hard work and intelligence and was a great organizer. The work culture was so different in Bombay from that in Kottayam. Fast pace of Bombay suited her temperament and the new responsibilities honed her skills further. Soon she had set up a fine office. Her uncle cum boss was immensely pleased with her efficient ways and gave her a hefty raise. She was in her mid-thirties and though surrounded with work, at times she felt very lonely. So when Verghese showed interest in her, she had no reservations in responding to his overtures. They liked each other; they understood and respected the need for individual space in their lives. It was not long before Verghese formally proposed to Mary and with a nod from the uncle, she accepted the proposal. They tied the knot in a simple ceremony. Her parents and sister flew down for the marriage; Verghese had no relations in India and his friends happily proxied for the missing relatives.

Mary had no difficulty in adjusting to the blissful married life. Verghese had a spacious apartment with adequate domestic help. Mary made a smooth transition in taking over one more responsibility of being a home maker. They were very happy together. Verghese was mild mannered; sensitive and considerate towards his spouse whom he admired and respected a lot. Mary continued with her job until Tracy arrived two years later.

Although her pregnancy had been uncomplicated, Mary's obstetrician felt a caesarian section was advisable due to her age. Tracy was a beautiful and healthy baby and Mary felt very proud and fulfilled when she held the baby for the first time. Verghese shared this wonderful moment of bliss with his wife in his usual understated manner that was so characteristic of him. Mary had given him all he could have asked for and he felt grateful to her. Mary had noticed that Verghese was trifle nervous and worried when he saw the little girl but passed it off as a routine paternal anxiety; specially at his age of 46 and when he had no prior experience of handling a new born!

Verghese in fact was worried as he had been told by the doctor that his new born daughter had an abnormal heart murmur and she might need further attention although there was no immediate cause to worry about. Mary was happy to come home accompanied by a new bundle of joy and she set her routine in her usual efficient manner setting apart quality time that she would still spend with Verghese. Since she had very good help at hand, she was confident that Verghese would have no reason to complain about any lack of attention now that the baby had arrived. They both were happy and grateful to the Lord Almighty.

Baby was formally named Tracy. Tracy was a glorious child, her deep-set black eyes were at a slant exaggerated by her chubby cheeks. With a jet-black curly head, she looked like a beautiful doll and her rosy lips were ever parted in a big smile even for strangers.

She did not cry much, a quality Mary and Verghese took as special concession for their advanced years of parenthood. Tracy used to catch cold easily and when this happened twice in a short spell, Verghese brought up the topic of the heart murmur that the doctor had told him about. She was now nearly four months old and since her cough and cold was not responding to the usual treatment, they decided to see a child specialist. By the time they got to the doctor, Tracy was running fever, her breathing was harsh and a bluish tinge could be easily made out on her otherwise rosy lips. The child specialist diagnosed this to be an attack of pneumonia and promptly put her on antibiotics. Once Tracy's infection was under control, he advised some more tests including an echocardiography. Mary was now worried and the child specialist shared his own concern with her as he suspected Tracy to have a defect in her heart, most probably a VSD or a hole in the heart.

As if this was not enough of a shock; he conveyed his suspicions that Tracy could also be a Mongoloid baby, also known as Down's syndrome. That was first time, either Mary or Verghese had heard of the term. But their nightmares had just started, they were now seeing one specialist after the other - regular pediatrician to a genetics expert, a cardiologist and finally a heart surgeon. Mary could not believe that her Tracy had any of the big named diseases that these doctors were busy labeling her with. Doctors were patient with them even as they put across the facts before them frankly but with compassion and asked them to prepare themselves for the ordeal ahead. Tracy was to have stunted physical and mental development, she was likely to catch respiratory and other infections more easily than other children did and a complicated structural defect inside her heart was only going to make it more difficult for her. One specialist told them in his well intentioned but wrongly placed bluntness that they should consider themselves lucky if Tracy 'succumbed to next episode of pneumonia 'as that could end their and Tracy's problems. He painted a gloomy picture of Tracy's future. "She probably would never be able to look after herself and would stretch your resources to an extreme. Even if she survived the heart operation, she could get a heart block needing a permanent pacemaker; besides she will continue to be mentally and physically challenged". Mary was dazed with medical advice coming thick and fast not only from the doctors but also from many friends and relatives. Tracy, special baby of Mary and Verghese had suddenly become a special baby for all. After several opinions and heart rendering details, they accepted the fact that Tracy indeed suffered from Down's syndrome and that she also had a complicated heart defect called A.V.Canal. Mary and Varghese had a long chat after coming back from the doctor's clinic, punctuated with several emotional breakdowns and finally resolved that they would not be put off by medical jargon. Tracy was God's special and precious gift to them, her Down's status notwithstanding. And they decided they would take care of Tracy for a long long time. Mary also decided that evening to direct all her managerial skills towards managing her baby. She quit her job although her uncle would have willingly allowed her the freedom of working from home.

She had made up her mind to give full time attention to Tracy. Mary started collecting all books that she could lay her hands on, about Down's syndrome. She collected articles, newspaper and magazine clippings. Her interaction with doctors, nurses and medical social workers looking after such children gave her valuable insights into the problems and special needs of such children. But Mary wanted to chart a different course, away from the beaten track of taking care of just basic needs of such individuals. She came to realize early that intelligence of these children varied a lot and if efforts were made early in infancy, it could certainly improve their skills and make them self-sufficient to a great extent. She learnt that somebody in the U. S. was advocating high doses of multi-vitamins, elsewhere others were working on developing mind-body co-ordinations and a few were experimenting with alternative medicine. Mary on the other hand, planned her own strategies and protocols to take care of Tracy's special needs. Her managerial skills were being tested and she decided that she would not fall short. The mission of her life was clearly focused in front of her and she knew that she had to achieve the goal in the shortest possible time.

Her spacious apartment looked more like a nursery or a kindergarten school, with brightly colored objects, toys, pictures scattered all over. Tracy was apparently enjoying the attention and seemed to be doing all right except that she seemed little slow in turning on her sides and was making no attempts at sitting or crawling. She was a pretty child and the neighborhood children adored her for Tracy had a special way with her broad smiles for all of them. Mary never restrained the children from playing with her or from carrying her outside except when she had cough and cold. Mary knew that Tracy caught infections easily and then required antibiotics for these to settle down. Otherwise she let Tracy face all the normal exposures to stimulate her just like any other child of her age and also make her cope up with teasing and pranks of her playmates just as she enjoyed the fuss that they made around her.

Tracy was unable to sit on her own even though she was six months of age while other kids at this age would be busy getting ready to crawl all over the place. Tracy seemed quite content when deposited at one place and played with toys lying around her. Mary would arrange a pile of cushions ensconcing Tracy as if on a throne only to find her little princess sliding down in no time or tumbling down on her side. She seemed to have such poor strength in her back and leg muscles. There were times of despair and disappointments for Mary but her pain and frustrations were, however, only transient as Tracy would give her a broad smile and Mary gained some more strength, some more courage. Mary had tremendous faith if not in her own abilities but definitely in the innocent purity of childhood, God would never allow Tracy to suffer in any way, she told herself whenever her own efforts seemed to flag down. Verghese was a strong supporter of her efforts. He chipped in whenever he could; his business had grown and he knew he needed to make more money to provide security for Tracy's future.

Tracy was operated upon for heart ailment when she was two years of age. The family and the doctor had decided that this would take care of her frequent respiratory infections and her physical condition was also likely to improve. The operation, fortunately, went all right except for some worry about heart block for a few days after the operation. The doctors had already warned them about this as the special pathway that carries electrical signals of the heart muscle runs very close to this type of defect and is, therefore, at danger. Fortunately the damage was not permanent and the temporary pacemaker wires fixed to an electric box outside took care of this episode. Mary and Verghese had been prepared for that eventuality. Tracy was favorite of all nurses and doctors in the Intensive Care Unit and later on in the ward also. Tracy was a happy child, she cried only when they came for blood tests. Mary was happy that her Tracy could give so much love and happiness to the people around her. Tracy had recovered from the operation and was well enough to be taken home after two weeks stay in the hospital. She needed little medication at home and was already eating better.

With the heart condition taken care of successfully, Mary started to concentrate her efforts on Tracy's physical development. She was careful in selecting her diet as Tracy had put on lot of weight and this could slow down her physical agility further. She substituted her favorite chocolates and pastries with fresh fruits. Only rule breaker in the house was Verghese. Mary had wondered how Tracy had special hug for Dad on his coming home from work until she discovered that Verghese would slip in a chocolate or some other goodie to Tracy. Mary did not protest although it was she who was running around her the entire day though liked to see Tracy's affections grow for her father, and it was also a pointer towards her mental growth. Tracy was crawling within a few months after her operation and could stand and even take a few bold steps by the time she celebrated her third birthday. It was lot slower than other kids were but it was some progress. Mary's next worry was about her education. Mary was teaching her simple alphabets, colors, shapes etc. at home but knew the difficulty they would have about admitting her in school. Mary had made some discrete inquiries and was told that while there should be no problem in the play school, the enrolment in a formal school may be extremely difficult. Mary and Verghese understood the problem but were enraged by the fact that those at the helm had precious little knowledge about Down's syndrome or for that matter any other physical or mental handicap and they made no effort to learn. Saying 'No' was so much easier option than empathize and understand the problems to be able to offer some sensitive solutions. It was at this stage that Mary intensified her efforts at home. She also tried to know about other parents in similar predicament. She went around again to the special clinics at the hospitals but her search was different from that of her earlier rounds of these clinics. In the beginning her purpose was to know from other parents as to how they had solved the problem for their children but she was taken aback when she saw their helplessness was even starker than hers. She found that her efforts at gaining all the knowledge by her reading and other interactions, had given her an edge and she decided to become a helping hand to others looking for change in the attitudes of so called normal individuals.

It was during one such visit that she met Sugandha. Sugandha's only son, Nilesh now 14, was diagnosed to have Down's syndrome when he was 8 months old. By the time Sugandha and her husband found out, she was already pregnant with her next child. Burdened with the anxiety and guilt about the unborn child being also abnormal, Sugandha tried to have an abortion at some ramshackle private clinic run by a quack. The abortion was botched and on being shifted to the medical college hospital after a considerable blood loss, her condition was precarious. She was saved but her uterus had to be removed during the emergency operation carried out to save her life.

Sugandha, already unhappy and guilty, became further frustrated when she learnt that she was unable to have any more children. Soon after, her husband left her for another woman and Nilesh neglected and reviled by his own parents, was continuously blamed for all the misfortunes. Short of deserting him, Sugandha gave no attention to the child except when she felt like venting her frustration by abusing him or beating him. Nilesh was oblivious to his mother's lack of attention or the abuse and made happy and affectionate gestures to her whenever she was in a better mood. She had found a low paid job to sweep and clean a doctor's dispensary in the morning and evening hours. Though the job did not pay well, there was no headache and the work was really not too much. She brought Nilesh with her and put him in a corner while she got busy with her work. Nilesh seemed to enjoy this outing and attracted attention of patients coming to the doctor's clinic. Finally the doctor convinced Sugandha to take him to the Down's children clinic at the hospital and even volunteered to talk to his pediatrician friend in charge of the clinic. This is where Mary met Sugandha during one of her many visits to the clinic. She noticed that most of the times Nilesh was left on his own to look after his needs and he did not seem to be doing too badly. That made an instant impression on Mary and when she discussed with the doctor, he confirmed what she had read that all such children could not be clubbed together. The physical as well as mental abilities of these children did vary from one another and while some children may be totally dependent on others for their most basic needs, others could be trained to acquire some degree of reasonable self-sufficiency. Mary decided to make Tracy, Nilesh and others like them to become independent, to enable them to take care of their routine care and also become a source of sharing and caring for each other. Ambitious she was, but not oblivious to the difficulties ahead; she believed that creation cannot always be a gentle expression, it was often rude and violent. And she prepared herself to absorb the violent shocks that would come her way. Her faith in God and her devout upbringing were great support and she felt deeply that it was Nilesh who was destined to lead her through this. For this, however, she had to bring Sugandha on her side. She became friends with her and offered her to come and work with her. She counseled and convinced Sugandha to get over her hostility towards her son, who was her own flesh and blood. She also taught her to accept him as creation of God, even if imperfect, with humility and graciousness. This counseling coming as it was from Mary, herself a mother of Down's child and herself having the tribulations and doubts of similar nature was a new experience for Sugandha. So far, she had received lot of pity and scorn but little understanding. Talking to Mary was a catharsis for Sugandha and she was suffused with new hope and happiness. She was feeling so much lighter now and when she held Nilesh in her arms, she noticed that there were innocent tears glistening in his clear eyes.

Mary now had new partners in Sugandha and Nilesh. Nilesh was very affectionate and protective towards Tracy. Mary, Sugandha, Tracy and Nilesh, a happy foursome, became an effective team as they encouraged others like them to join their group and explore new joy and happiness. Thus a support group for Down's children was born in Mary's apartment when a couple of parents and children who they had met in the special clinics, trooped in her apartment and asked if they could join them!

They started meeting every Saturday afternoon; both parents were encouraged to attend these meetings whenever it was possible. Since most of these individuals came from low middle class, Mary and Varghese saw to it that their affluence did not intimidate anyone. They genuinely wanted to help those who were less fortunate and less privileged than themselves. Caring and sharing became the common thread to spread the joy and happiness that radiated from the faces of the innocent children but more on the faces of parents and friends who came for these meetings in increasing numbers. Mary's apartment, though large, was becoming small to hold these meetings and they had to look for space outside. 'The place should be accessible easily and also should be able to accommodate the future needs', Mary told Varghese. Varghese agreed to part with his large warehouse in the city and told his manager to get the place ready with fresh paint and furniture.

Mary registered her support group as a charitable trust with personal donation of her own savings. Settling on name for the organization took a little time because Mary was inclined to name the organization after Tracy but Verghese did not have to work very hard to persuade her to keep a more general name. He did not wish to hurt feelings of those who could not chip in financially. 'They should not feel small or have sense of belonging any less than Tracy', he told Mary gently but firmly. Finally it was a collective exercise of many heads when they finally settled on "Foundation for Rehabilitation for Down's children". FORD, the acronym was rather elitist but impressive all the same. FORD was established on fifth birthday of Tracy and now ten years later, had a substantial reputation and membership. Nilesh was the motivator and besides him and Tracy, there were thirty other children of different ages registered with the foundation. Donations, endowments small and big, came along and the finances were secure even if not overflowing. Mary and Verghese had worked very hard collecting funds and charting the activities of the foundation. They had eventually planned to donate all their belongings including the house they lived in to the foundation. Mary's uncle not only donated big sums of money himself but also championed the cause whenever in big meetings at home or abroad. He often teased Mary that her empire was bigger than his business. The apartment could house Tracy, Nilesh and

Sugandha after Mary and Verghese left the scene. And FORD will continue to support many other children by advocating for the inclusion of children with Down syndrome into the general school system, for a greater understanding of the condition among the general population and providing support for families with children with Down syndrome.

DAUGHTERS ARE YOUR SHADOWS...

Technology has been a transformational force in many fields including medicine. It is a double edged sword, easy to be misused like in prenatal sex determination of the fetus. Indians have preference for sons and lately there has been focus on 'missing girls.' Sex selective abortions have led to undesirable sex ratio of 925 girls to 1000 boys or even worse in some states like Haryana and Punjab.. Also there is a growing trend in the western countries to abort the fetus with complex anomalies diagnosed in utero. There are ethical issues involved in medical termination of pregnancy and there are bound to be many differing opinions. Besides the moral, ethical and economic implications to the parents and society, such choices can scar the soul of women and some times fracture delicate relationships.

I first met Sushila in my clinic when she and her husband brought Aayush, their year and half old son, for his heart ailment. Aayush also had mild hydrocephalus and significant deformity of feet (clubfeet). He had been referred for heart surgery by the orthopaedic surgeon, as the corrective surgery for his feet could not be performed unless his heart condition was fixed. Sushila and her husband looked extremely distraught and unhappy. This was understandable as the mere thought of heart surgery on an infant would unsettle any parent. Besides, the harassment of running from one doctor to another, getting various tests completed and meeting the expenses could test anyone's patience. They appeared rather old for such a young child as I tried to guess their age to be in mid forties. I was saved the embarrassment of asking as Sushila volunteered that he was their *only* son born after three daughters. Her eldest daughter was seventeen years old. My contemptuous outburst against yet another instance of elusive happiness that only a son could give was checked by their very sad expressions. Later when I was examining Aayush, I again felt distracted by Sushila. An air of melancholy hung around her persona; her eyes were down cast and a shadow of sadness spread across her face. Her husband stood in the corner, as there was only one stool in the small OPD where Sushila sat with Aayush in her lap. His expression, though a little less strident was not very different. As I looked more closely at her, I realized that Sushila must have been quite good looking when young. Her oval face was thin and pale with dark circles around her large eyes but her features were still very sharp. I asked her age and she told me that she really did not remember her age but should be around thirty-six or thirty-seven. I explained to them about the heart disease of their son. They seemed well informed by the family doctor. Since the child had already been fully investigated and worked up, I discussed about the operation and the likely expenses for it and directed them to see the medical social worker. They requested for an early appointment, as they did not need any financial assistance. I assured them that in that case it should be possible to take him for surgery in the following week. Sushila's face did not leave my thoughts long after she was gone. I kept thinking about her as I tried to fathom what her face was conveying to me. There was something troubling about her masking the undercurrents of pain and anguish written large over her face. These extended beyond the worries about the impending heart surgery of their son.

Sushila and her husband had deposited the money in the hospital and Aayush was admitted for surgery. I had a chance to study Sushila closely as she was staying with Aayush all the time. She was very quiet and never asked too many questions. It was usual for the patients and their families to bond well under stress but Sushila kept mostly to herself, tending to her son. I observed her moods from close quarters and felt that her emotions were a mix of pain, guilt, remorse, self-pity, and an unexplained sadness. I was intrigued when even after Aayush was operated upon successfully, there was not much rejoicing on her face although she was obviously relieved. She listened quietly as I told her that now that his heart had been fixed, the operation for the correction of deformity would be quite simple and I could request the orthopaedic surgeon for an early appointment. She gave a grateful but very reserved smile before going back into her shell. Her husband was by her side most of the time and no one had noticed any friction between them. This only made me more curious and I was determined to find out and help if I could. The ward sister told me that whenever her husband could not come, her daughter brought her meals. She had also noticed that her daughter's visits left Sushila disturbed and very sad. I asked the nurse to let me know when the daughter came in. May be she could help me in solving the puzzle. I also told Sushila to ask her daughter to see me as Aayush was likely to be discharged from the hospital soon and I needed to give some instructions to the family. Same evening, Sushila and her daughter came to my office. Saloni was around seventeen or eighteen and had taken the good looks of her mother. She was tall and lissome; with her sharp features and large kohl lined eyes, Sushila must have looked like Saloni when she was her age. Saloni was soft spoken and heard me out politely. She seemed to be an intelligent girl with no overt sign of any conflict as she asked some pertinent questions about her brother's next operation. At the same time I sensed a certain coolness between the mother and daughter. Saloni muttered soft thanks and left. This was when Sushila broke down.

Mother and daughter had shared a very close relationship but that was till a few years ago. Lately Saloni had grown aloof and had drifted away from the mother. She was still civil towards her but there was no warmth. Sushila was unable to understand the cause of strange looks that she thought Saloni gave her these days; Sushila did not even know what these looks conveyed; anger or hatred, disgust or loathfulness, or was it plain pity! Sushila had initially tried to ask Saloni about her changed behavior but Saloni had totally ignored her. It was this in-difference of her daughter that distressed her so much. Sushila finished what she had to say and her face was washed with tears. she now seemed calm having unburdened her grief. I could only murmur that things would sort out soon. I also promised Sushila that I would talk with Saloni.

I tried to cultivate Saloni and called her over whenever I stayed late in the hospital. We talked of different subjects and sometimes, I would ask her to do odd jobs for me that she seemed to like doing. I found her to be a very sensitive young girl, who had grown into a woman very fast and yet retained the innocence; she was quick to respond to any friendly gesture. She continued to see me even after Aayush was transferred to the orthopaedic ward for surgery. After several sessions of my interaction with Sushila and Saloni, their story unfolded.

Sushila was married to Karsanbhai before she had turned eighteen. Karsanbhai hailed from the same village but had moved over to Mumbai along with his father and uncles, who were working there as tailors. They had rich clients from Malabar hill and Napean Sea road and had set up shop in the same area. Karsanbhai had been quick to learn the tricks of the trade at a young age and soon with his hard work and intuitive business sense, had set up an independent shop. There was lot of hard work but the money too was good. After marriage, he had brought Sushila to this shop only until he found a room close by. Karsanbhai was a good husband and took great care of his gentle and beautiful wife. They were happy and felt blessed as they set up their home together. Sushila helped him with odd jobs like putting hooks and buttons or at times even with the designs. That was until their elder daughter, Saloni, arrived within a year of their marriage. Second daughter, Bhairavi, was born two years after Saloni. Their lives were full with the two lovely daughters and they rejoiced watching them grow. They had celebrated every milestone of Saloni and even that of Bhairavi to some extent.

Sushila sometime would visit clients' homes to deliver the stitched clothes. She had observed with keen interest how beautiful and rich women lived in their palatial homes and conversed smartly in English. Sushila would dream of sending her daughters to the English medium school. Karsanbhai managed to save some dress materials to stitch pretty dresses for children whenever he could like whenever she was going to the village for the Navratri festival. She and her daughters had drawn admiring and envious looks of the relatives. Sushila's happiness, however, was short lived and she feverishly packed to come back. Saloni and Bhairavi, at six and four years respectively, were unable to understand why their mother was upset and wanted to go back to Mumbai when they were having a gala time in the village. Sushila had had some plain speak from her in-laws for not having a son even after seven years of her marriage. They were also critical about the manner they were bringing up the girls. Sushila could only manage to get angry and frustrated with herself for not having courage to tell them that she and her husband were perfectly happy with their two daughters.

Karsanbhai heard the story on her return from the village but with out the outrage felt by his wife. Sushila was hurt even more by his feeble response. A letter arrived from the village soon after and Sushila could see Karsanbhai looking worried and pensive after that. Initially he refused to tell Sushila anything about the contents of the letter. When she persisted, Karsanbhai told her that Ba and Bapuji were very perturbed after her visit and if she did not give birth to a son, they had threatened to get him married again. Sushila was left gaping after hearing this; her lips quivered to say something but no words escaped her lips. Another blow awaited Sushila when he told her soon after that he was not interested in sending Saloni and Bhairavi to the English medium school as they were not looking for any career and they would need money for their weddings too. Sushila felt she had failed yet again as the girls were admitted in a Gujarati medium school near by without any sembelance of resistance on her part.

Meanwhile Sushila found herself pregnant again. She was surprised at herself praying for a son this time. Karsanbhai was also excited, as he was sure that this time, it would be a son. Even the girls were preparing to receive a baby brother with much anticipation. The vibrant mood was replaced by heavy disappointment when Sushila gave birth to yet another girl. Sushila and Karsanbhai were in low spirits when they informed their relatives about the new arrival. Saloni was the only person in the house whose spirits were not dampened as she fondled her little sister. Even at her tender age of seven years, Saloni was sensitive enough to understand that somehow her little sister was not welcome. This made her very protective about her sister, who was named Paulomi without any fanfare. Karsanbhai's mother was expected to come and help out but she now cancelled her trip. Meanwhile as Sushila was finding it difficult to manage alone, it was decided that she should visit her mother's place for sometime. It did not seem to matter that it was the middle of the school term. Saloni was not happy to miss school like this but Bhairavi was game and looking forward to fun-filled days ahead.

Once at her mother's house, Sushila got much needed rest. Her sister-in-law loved Saloni and Bhairavi and would take care of Paulomi too. Sushila was feeling stronger and cheerful but worried about her husband being alone. She told her mother to send her back even though Karsanbhai was supposed to come and fetch her a little later. Sushila's mother was a wise and pragmatic woman and did not wish Sushila to stay away from her husband for long. She knew that Karsanbhai and his parents were very unhappy about Sushila having only girls. So before Sushila left for Mumbai, she advised Sushila to observe several fasts and special prayers so that her next child would definitely be a son.

Karsanbhai was happy when Sushila and children came back as he was finding it really difficult with out them. The girls went back to the school. Sushila was doing her best to cope though felt tired at the end of the day. As the pressure of work had increased for Karsanbhai also, he was getting irritable and scolded her for little things. He would find faults with her cooking and housekeeping. Everytime Paulomi cried, Sushila had to rush to quiten her, leaving whatever else she might be doing as her continued crying would make Karsanbhai to lose his temper. It was not only crying Paulomi that got him angry these days but playful shrieks and laughter of the girls also disturbed him. Soon Sushila herself was getting upset with her daughters on small pretexts. Saloni's sensibilities were being metamorphosed due to increasing tensions at home and she had grown quiet and introverted. She would often run to pick up Paulomi as soon as she started to cry leaving her books aside and take her out. She was only nine and constantly thinking of ways to please her parents. Bhairavi on the other hand was becoming more rebellious and boisterous and had become quite a bully. Sushila found it extremely difficult to control her tantrums but fortunately she listened to Saloni. Paulomi, though the center of all chaos, was oblivious to everything happening around her as she waddled around filling the house with her happy shrieks, specially when she saw Saloni.

Sushila and Karsanbhai were growing anxious to have a son and as the days passed, their craving for the son only increased. The barbs and the whispers of the relatives and friends had given them tremendous complex especially to Sushila. She now more than Karsanbhai wanted a son at all costs and was visiting doctors, hakims and the sooth-sayers. It was not that they were unaware of the burden of feeding one more mouth. Though Karsanbhai made good money, they were finding it difficult to run the house. Saloni and Bhairavi were not in expensive schools, but required something or the other everyday. Paulomi caused them no expense as dresses and toys of older girls were handed down to her but she would be going to school shortly and one more child would definitely stretch their resources further. But if it were a son, this might not hurt or so they thought. They even believed that the son would bring them luck beside rich gifts of cash and gold from relatives.

Waliben was Sushila's neighbour and knew about the turmoil in her friend's life. So next time, Sushila was pregnant, she told her about a new test available whereby she could know in advance whether it was a boy or a girl. She further comforted Sushila that if it was a girl, the doctor in the clinic could even help her in getting rid of the pregnancy. Sushila gasped, she had never before heard of such a test ('amniocentesis'). She was not sure how Karsanbhai would react to Waliben's advice and decided not to tell him just then. Karsanbhai was going to the village for a few days and Sushila decided to go to Dr. Kothari's clinic along with Waliben.

She entered the clinic with a pounding heart accompanied by Waliben. The nurse looked at her without any interest as she mechanically motioned her to wait for her turn. Sushila noticed with some relief that there were three other women waiting to see the doctor as she settled down nervously on a small grimy sofa in the waiting room. Sushila wondered if these other women also had three daughters at home like she had and if they were all there for a common cause. The doctor was a middle aged plumpish lady; her round eyes quickly sized Sushila as she entered her cabin. By this time, Sushila's heartbeat had quickened further and her mouth had gone dry. She had a strong urge to run away. Even as she was grappling with her thoughts, Waliben nudged her gently towards the examination table. The doctor examined her and the test was over before Sushila knew about it. All this time, neither the doctor nor the nurse had asked her any question; they had explained nothing as if they knew the purpose of her visit to the clinic. "May be Waliben had already talked to them and they did not wish to embarrass her further", Sushila told herself. Sushila was relieved that the test was not painful. She was asked to bring three thousand rupees and collect the report after 48 hours. On seeing the alarmed expression on her face, the nurse explained that the charges included the fee for an abortion if one was needed. Sushila felt sick in the stomach as she was escorted home by Waliben.

Sushila remained nervous and fidgety during next two days. Saloni made simple meals and fed her sisters even as she worried that mother was not looking well. She gently inquired but Sushila shooed her away. The day Sushila was to collect the report, she had a long session of prayers at the local temple on her way to the doctor's clinic. Sushila was surprised to see that Waliben was already in the clinic when she reached there. But it was her facial expression that panicked Sushila. She turned pale when the nurse confirmed that the amniocentesis test had shown her to be pregnant with a girl child yet again. She had not even recovered from the initial shock when the doctor appeared briefly to ask if she had come prepared for the termination of pregnancy. Sushila's mind was racing fast, a fourth daughter would seal her fate completely; Karsanbhai might also agree for getting married again as it was question of having a male heir in the family. He was away for another two full days and she wondered if she should wait for him to come back. She was hesitant to make such a big decision without asking him. Waliben read her thoughts and convinced her how quick and safe the procedure was. She named practically every woman from the neighbourhood whom she had helped in getting rid of an unwanted pregnancy in the doctor's clinic. There was a glint of pride in her eyes but Sushila was too pre-occupied to notice it. Waliben volunteered to negotiate the doctor's fee and to take care of Paulomi. Prodded and persuaded by Waliben, Sushila agreed, only pleading with her friend to keep her secret safe! Sushila returned home before Saloni and Bhairavi were back from the school. The operation had left her a little weak but also greatly relieved. She even felt secretly happy that first time since her marriage, she had taken a decision with out asking her husband. But soon the guilt was over riding as she watched little Paulomi cuddling to her- had she known about this test before Paulomi was born, may be... a chill ran through her spine.

Karsanbhai came back from the village and on finding a suitable moment, Sushila confided in him about the entire episode. He did not appear to be annoyed but kept quiet. Sushila had two more abortions in the following years and with Karsanbhai's unconditional acquiescence on both the occasions. Sushila had become so confident that second time, she went to the clinic without Waliben, a fact that latter had deeply resented. Technology, meanwhile, had progressed and ultrasound machines were around making prenatal sex determination simple and available even in remote places. Sushila and Karsanbhai had become co-conspirators in their insatiable quest for a son and if they had felt guilty earlier, there was now a false sense of security and expectancy. The thoughts of immorality or gender bias did not ever cross their minds. It was as if their mind-space was fully occupied by the centuries old collective consciousness where a son was a must for their *Moksha*. They were also not bothered that repeated pregnancies and abortions had taken a heavy toll on Sushila's health. She had grown thinner, was anaemic and tired easily. Her beauty and verve, that used to drive Karsanbhai crazy, were things of the past. Karsanbhai himself had grown thinner and was looking older under the constant worry of running the house. This had also meant a gradual transfer of household burden on the tender shoulders of Saloni. She would often miss her school so as to cook and clean for the family. She silently carried on taking care of her siblings too as Sushila was finding it more and more difficult to look after the house and the kids. But Bhairavi was becoming more rebellious. She answered back the mother whenever confronted or asked to help in the household chores though Saloni still had a calming influence on her. Little Paulomi was cruising along unaware that she was the epicenter of the storm brewing around her. Karsanbhai remained irritable whenever he was at home; he was unable to finish the orders in time and was not keeping up with the new trends. He blamed Sushila and the children for his failing business.

All this, however, had not diminished their desire to have a son. So next time she became pregnant, they visited the shrines of all faiths to propitiate all gods as if not wanting to take any chances. They performed more pujas and Sushila wore more charms when she went for the Sonography test. They were in for a long cherished and welcome surprise this time; overjoyed though they were, both found it hard to believe when the doctor told them that this time it was a boy! They asked the doctor to doubly confirm before the news could sink in. Sushila was crying in an unabashed manner as the pain and taunts of not having a male child instantly melted away. She felt one amongst the equals after what was an agonizing wait. Even Karsanbhai felt a new vitality in his otherwise dull life. He ignored the streaks of grey in his hair as he fussed around Sushila as if she was going to have her first child. Saloni felt withdrawn while her sisters were delighted as the mood in the household cheered up. This also meant more burden on delicate shoulders of Saloni. It was taken for granted that she would take care of home and the siblings and her school was just incidental. She was unhappy as she had already fallen behind by two years. Saloni was now seventeen and had good looks of the mother; her own emotions unfolding everyday before her. She kept aloof from the ecstatic preparations being made for Sushila's delivery. This was also the time when Sushila noticed Saloni giving her strange looks. Sushila told Karsanbhai about this and both of them wondered if Saloni knew about the abortions or the reasons for the same. Sushila had been discreet but still could not be sure.

Saloni in fact had known all along, from the first time till the last. She had overheard the several conversations between her mother and Waliben. Saloni's innocent mind had been confounded by several doubts but she could not ask her mother for any clarifications. She did not know that even if she had dared to ask, there were any answers for her questions as to why the girl child was killed even before she was born. She was angry with her mother and thought how she could, herself a woman, agree to killing her unborn daughters? Her mother was not a total illiterate having gone to the school before she got married but her education seemed so useless to Saloni since it had not educated her in getting over the bias and complex of not having a son. Her emotions vacillated from anger to pity and at times contempt for her mother. She herself felt diminished in some way. The distance between mother and daughter kept growing as Sushila's pregnancy advanced.

Finally the son was born and soon the house was over running with the relatives and friends celebrating the event. There were presents not only for the newborn but also for the entire family. For a change Bhairavi was sober and happy and enjoying even as Saloni kept herself aloof from the festivities. The gold earrings that Sushila gave her failed to buy peace between them. Little boy, oblivious of all the fuss made around him, was named Aayush.

Life returned to normal as the guests departed. Karsanbhai knew that he needed to work harder and make more money but now Aayush, his son was the incentive. He would hire some help and get more work. He felt more energetic and was dreaming how he would expand the shop by the time his son grew up. Saloni was staying away from school more frequently as Sushila got busy with the massage and feeds of her little prince who was now the focus of her affection and attention.

Aayush was nearly four months of age when the doctors noticed his head was a little larger than the normal. Also his feet were curved inwards and it was realized that he would be unable to stand or walk because of "club feet". The orthopaedic surgeon in the children's hospital had advised multiple operations to set the deformity right. It was, however, the anaesthetist who first noticed the bluish tinge of the lips during a pre-operative check and asked for an opinion from a heart specialist. Sushila did not believe any of what the doctor was telling her and took him home. Aayush was meanwhile running fever and this time Sushila too noticed the bluish discoloration of his lips; he was rushed to the hospital where he had a convulsion and needed to be on oxygen for several days. The world had turned topsy-turvy for Sushila and Karsanbhai. They both felt shattered and wondered how could their joy be so short lived. Once his condition improved, further tests were carried out, these revealed that Aayush had a congenital birth defect of the heart called Tetralogy of Fallot. There was a serious malformation inside the heart with a large hole along with much reduced blood flow to the lungs. It was made abundantly clear to them that unless something was done for the heart defect, no operation could be carried out on Aayush's feet. The anxiety and concern for their little child were now mixed with guilt and remorse. Sushila and Karsanbhai were constantly haunted by the thoughts of all the prenatal tests and the multiple abortions she had undergone. They were convinced this to be a retribution for their sins. But that little Aayush should suffer for their sins was difficult to contend with. They made several rounds of the children's hospital from orthopaedic to cardiology experts. This had affected Karsanbhai's work and the income was dwindling fast. The home was now entirely looked after by Saloni and no one even noticed when she dropped out of the school. No one had really asked her to do so but it was her own sensitive nature that she decided not to go to the school anymore. This was the story so far of a serious drift in their relationship; mother and daughter grew distant, cold and sad in their own private worlds.

By the time Aayush had made good recovery after his cardiac surgery, Saloni had had several sessions talking about her trauma. My colleague from the psychiatry department willingly chipped in with her time. I could see Saloni's anger against her parents getting replaced with loving sadness for both of them. She fondly remembered, while chatting with me one evening, how her parents had rejoiced when Aayush was born and how unhappy his illness had made all of them. Even Bhairavi had mellowed by the tragic events at home and was seen helping Saloni. It was only Paulomi who made them laugh as she asked them with all innocence of her five years, if mummy was getting them another brother from the hospital!

After a few weeks of his heart surgery, Aayush was operated upon for the deformity of his feet. And finally he was allowed to go home as Sushila prepared confidently for a battle of conscience with her daughter. She was thrilled as Saloni welcomed her parents and little brother with a broad smile. She looked at her mother with tenderness and affection before taking her in a loving embrace. Saloni was hugging and kissing her mother and Aayush as she had understood the pain her mother had gone through. Sushila and Karsanbhai hoped that both God and their daughter had forgiven them. Looking on innocently was little Aayush with his eyes sparkling and a soft smile playing on his rosy lips.

Saloni would finish the high school with Karsanbhai willingly paying for her tuitions. Sushila was happy that though it took a trial by fire and lot of suffering but she had got rid of her demons; her daughter was empowered to make the right choices in her own life. She was confident that Saloni would think different and do different.

For me, Saloni's liberation was a bigger award than the successful heart operation of her brother.

LIFE IS A JOURNEY...
just a little longer and difficult in the life of a woman with heart disease

Rheumatic heart disease is almost non-existent in most developed nations. The disease ebbed not so much due to availability of Penicillin but due to improved sanitation and living conditions with fast changing socio-economic conditions. The disease usually starts with streptococcal throat infection and ends up ravaging the heart valves if untreated. According to WHO rheumatic fever (RF) and rheumatic heart disease (RHD) incidence is still extremely high in the developing countries. Nearly 400,000 deaths occur due to RF and its heart complications. The global burden of the disease is estimated at a high 1% of school children. This is most common in the four geographic areas of Asia, Africa, South Americas, and East Mediterranean region. Disease occurs amongst the poorest in these regions that find even a single monthly injection of Penicillin unaffordable. Further since the disease affects the poor and the young, it directly impacts the youth who are the future economic assets. Economic aspects of the disease are more profound when many do not return to a fully productive life even after expensive heart surgery. The young girls and women face stringent social pressures in addition to the discomfort of disease once stigmatized as heart patients.

Story of Aruna is only symptomatic of wide spread abuse of such women or even worse.....while Aruna made her journey of life with courage unusual for a middle class Indian woman, many Arunas lose their way without getting a second chance.

This story also describes open heart surgery for a heart valve replacement as carried out some 30 years back.

Aruna sat in the chair, a large glass-topped table in front of her, for the last time. The table was bereft of all papers. She had only a few framed certificates, personal awards and memorabilia in front of her. President's medal for best teacher awarded to her a few years back, a gleaming and shining silver salver, multiple bouquets of flowers and some lonely roses were tearful farewell of the students and staff to their much loved and adored principal. She packed these certificates and awards in a small bag with gentle care and soft touch of affection. There was a story of her triumphs and tears behind the shimmer of these awards and gentle fragrance of the flowers. Her chain of thoughts was broken by a tall and lanky young man standing in the doorway and calling out to her, "Ma, are you all done up! Let us leave, you have to catch a train and station is some distance from here." She smiled, wiping her tears, as she got up to hug her son, Amar. Amar had already put her bags in the boot of his car. She looked at the school and then at her cottage longingly and got in the car besides Amar. The car sped away towards Pune railway station. The air was cool and crisp. Aruna closed her eyes and the story of her life flashed past like an unwinding spool of film.

Aruna had had a typical life in her middle class parents' house, located in a small town, Dhule, in Maharashtra. She was third amongst four daughters and two sons of Ramlal and Sumitra. Sumitra's personal experiences as a woman had in no way influenced her own preference for the sons. It was not as if she was not fond of her daughters. She brought them up lovingly and made sure that they learnt all the household chores, an attribute that she believed to be essential for ultimate happiness in their married life. She, however, chided Ramlal for encouraging the girls to get educated and that too in city college. She had told him on umpteen occasions that she wished to see them married and settled before he retired as a headmaster from the high school. The boys were not exactly boorish, though they did not mind the extra attention of the mother. The sisters were clever and had smartly distributed the work amongst them; the division of labour had helped them to keep the mother happy and at the same time leave enough time for the studies too. As the girls grew up, Ramlal seemed to go along the advice of his wife and started looking for suitable grooms for his daughters. Aruna was the most intelligent amongst siblings and Ramlal secretly wished her to get higher education. He knew that she too was interested in studying further but felt helpless in face of limited resources as also 'wifely' pressure. Aruna herself sensitive to the monetary constraints of the family, did not protest much when married off after she passed out from the high school, like her sisters had been before her.

Aruna's husband, Jagtap, had a good government job in the revenue department and lived comfortably in nearby town of Nashik with his parents.

Aruna settled down to her new life with Jagtap. At an opportune time, she cautiously told Jagtap that she wished to pursue her studies. She knew that it would not be possible for her to join the college as a regular student but it should not be a problem to take the examinations as a private student. She was pleasantly surprised and thankful when Jagtap did not oppose the idea as long as Aruna managed the household responsibilities well and took proper care of his parents. Aruna took her studies seriously. She collected the information about distance education and planned her time meticulously. But this resulted in lot of running around even as she carefully balanced this with her domestic chores. It was during this time that she noticed that she was feeling very tired and having difficulty in breathing, especially after finishing cleaning and washing jobs. She blamed it on the fact that the work at her parents' house was neatly divided amongst four of them whereas now she had to do everything by herself. Her books were getting neglected in the process but she could not help it. Her symptoms kept progressing and she was short of breath most of the time even as she carried out simple routine activities. To her horror, she also realised that she was two months pregnant. There was some swelling on her face and around her ankles and she was finding it difficult to lie down flat in the bed. As she finished her chores and retired to bed, she would start feeling choked; she could feel her heart pounding very hard inside her chest.

Jagtap took her to see the family doctor who initially prescribed some medicines and injections. The doctor advised her to undergo some more tests including echocardiography as he suspected that she was suffering from rheumatic heart disease made worse with pregnancy; one of the four heart valves, mitral valve, seemed to be leaking significantly. She was feeling better with the medicines and could not comprehend exactly what the doctor had meant by mitral valve disease even as she underwent the ultrasound and 2-D Echocardiography as advised by the doctor. The reports confirmed both her pregnancy and the heart disease. By this time, she was already in the fourth month of her pregnancy. The doctor warned her that she could continue the pregnancy with some risk provided she took the medication properly. But should her symptoms get worse, she might require an intervention as otherwise it could be dangerous to her life. As they returned home, Jagtap told Aruna not to tell his mother at least till they had sorted out what should be done.

Aruna had had no major illness till then and was shocked to hear that she had heart disease. The doctor had asked her if she had any joint pains while she was young and she thought of asking her father when she met him next. She felt she could carry on as before while taking her medicines regularly. The household responsibilities, however, left hardly any time for her to rest as her mother-in-law kept her busy with something or the other. Over next few weeks, her condition took a turn for the worse and she had to be admitted in the hospital. The doctor insisted that she took complete rest if she wanted to continue with the pregnancy. It was during this time that she found a sudden change in the attitude of Jagtap and his parents towards her. Jagtap had quietly confided in his mother about her heart ailment and she in turn squarely blamed Aruna's parents for concealing her illness from them. Jagtap too seemed to believe his mother and came to the hospital only occasionally to see her. Whenever she confronted him, he would offer some excuse or the other, of being busy with his office work. Meanwhile her in-laws had stopped coming to the hospital and even as she was responding to the treatment and her pregnancy was continuing normally, she remained very unhappy and lonely. She was sure that her father did not know about her having a serious heart disease; had he known about it, he would not hide it from her or from any one else. She requested Jagtap, when he came to see her after a gap of few days, to inform her parents about her being in the hospital. In turn Jagtap suggested that he could take her to her parents' house as soon as she was released from the hospital. This way she could meet her family and also get proper rest and medical attention too. Aruna agreed but when she expressed her desire to seek permission from her in-laws, Jagtap admonished her and told her that this was not necessary. Aruna knew that her going away like this was not proper and could be used against her but felt too weak to continue the argument further.

She left for Dhule along with Jagtap directly from the hospital. Her parents and her brothers were delighted to see her but were alarmed to see her rundown condition. News of Aruna's pregnancy elated their spirits. Her younger sister, who was married and living in the same town, came to see them. She was very fond of Jagtap and they used to get along fine but this time she sensed something amiss in his behaviour. Jagtap left the same night and it was only after he left that Aruna told them how the events had unfolded for her after her marriage. Ramlal was extremely concerned about her illness and her future but Sumitra told him in her worldly-wise way that once the baby came along, all would be well. She had probably not understood that Aruna had a serious heart problem and her life as also that of the baby were at great risk. Ramlal and her younger sister took her to the hospital in Dhule where the doctor explained to them that she must have suffered rheumatic fever in childhood although they could not recall it. It was during this episode that her heart valve had been affected and he suspected that the orifice of the valve was narrowed to some extent besides having a significant leakage. He further opined that though her condition was under control, she could run into difficulty anytime and it would be safer for her to go to Mumbai for delivery. He told them that one of his classmates was a senior cardiologist in the King Edward Memorial hospital and he could write a note to him. He further assured them that the KEM hospital had a reputed cardiac unit and Aruna would be well looked after over there.

Ramlal sent a message to Jagtap but as Aruna had expected, there was no response from his side. Aruna's pregnancy advanced into last month amidst visits to the doctors, medicines and increasing doubts about her marriage and the outcome of the pregnancy. She had thought that her first pregnancy would be an occasion to rejoice like it had been with her sisters and friends but things had gone wrong for her, awfully wrong. She worried about her heart failing as the baby came and if she did not survive, who would look after the baby? She remained depressed and anxious but as was her nature, she kept her worries to herself.

As there was no news from Jagtap, and the doctor was insisting that she go to Mumbai before it was too late, Ramlal asked his younger daughter and her husband to accompany them to the city. He had visited Mumbai only once before this and felt greatly intimidated as they alighted from the train at Dadar station. It was crowded and they were jostled and pushed around as they found their way out. They reached the hospital and saw crowds of unfamiliar faces all around; Ramlal felt his pocket and felt reassured with the letter that the referring doctor had given for the heart specialist. They were directed to go to the cardiac outpatients department. There were patients every where while doctors and nurses looked very busy as they rushed in and out.

Meanwhile the strain of long journey had exhausted Aruna completely; she was leaning against her sister and was having extreme difficulty in breathing. While Ramlal and her brother-in-law were desperately trying to locate the doctor, her sister was frightened to see Aruna sinking in her arms. Her breathing had become very shallow, her colour was pale almost ashen and her hands felt very cold. She was soon losing consciousness as her sister cradled her in her arms and that drew the attention of a young resident doctor who was passing by. He just called out to the nurse to get the stretcher as he and the nurse rushed her to the emergency room. The nurse pulled the oxygen mask on her face and helped the doctor in searching for a vein on the back of her hand. Ramlal, Aruna's sister and brother-in law were asked out of the treatment room but not before they heard the junior doctor cursing them under his breath for bringing a dying patient to the hospital. A needle had been thrust in a vein in her arm and intravenous injections of Lasix and Aminophyllin were shouted for and given promptly. She had been hooked on to a cardiac monitor while another nurse had hung up a Dopamine drip. The doctor, who had rushed to Aruna on seeing her in the waiting room, signalled Ramlal to accompany him in the elevator and told others to take the stairs to the fourth floor. As they were moving up in the elevator, his hand continuously feeling Aruna's feeble pulse, he told Ramlal that the patient's condition was extremely serious; if she did not deliver naturally they may have to operate upon her and that their first priority would be to save the life of mother. Even otherwise baby could have suffered some brain damage due to lack of oxygen in the condition that Aruna had reached the hospital. Ramlal was still clutching at the letter given by the family doctor but lacked courage to give the same to the doctor, as he grappled to understand what the doctor was telling him.

Once Aruna was settled in the intensive care unit, the nurse pushed a sheaf of papers including the consent form for operation in front of Ramlal. He signed with a trembling hand as directed but without understanding what was written therein and no one bothered to explain. He was nervous and hoping that Jagtap would come fast and share the responsibility. Aruna's sister stayed back with the father while her husband was despatched with her gold bangles to arrange for some more money. Fortunately Aruna had responded favourably to the intensive medications along with the efforts of the doctors, and she delivered a baby boy without further complications. Once the baby was delivered, there was remarkable improvement in Aruna's condition. She still needed to be kept under observation in the ICU and the dopamine drip was continued, her heartbeat was getting stabilised and the relieved doctors told the that them worse was over. The baby was lucky too, as he had escaped any brain damage due to lack of oxygen in the period preceding his birth!

Jagtap arrived soon after; he was annoyed that he had been informed so late and that too when he was in an important meeting with the minister. Ramlal was apologetic as he explained how they had to leave at a short notice and how critical Aruna's condition was when they reached the hospital. Jagtap left soon after without saying as to when he would return.

Since she was making good recovery, she was discharged from the hospital, after a few days observation in the general ward. She was advised to continue medications against heart failure and was warned against another pregnancy before her heart disease was fixed. She had already been seen by the cardiac surgeon and advised replacement of the diseased heart valve. A second pregnancy could be fatal for her!

Jagtap had come on brief visits while she was in the hospital but had brought little cheer to Aruna. He often mentioned about the difficulty he was having in looking after his parents because of her illness. Since her condition was still very weak and she would be unable to take care of the household and the baby, it was decided that she returned to her parents' home for some more time. Her sister stayed on for a few more days to help her. She along with her husband had been of great help and support for which Aruna was gratefully embarrassed.

Since the baby had had a providential life, he was aptly named Amar. Her other two sisters too visited her in turns. Sumitra was happy to take care of her grandson. Aruna, meanwhile, worried as no one from her in-laws' house had come to see her or the new-born. So as soon as she felt strong enough, she told Sumitra about her desire to go back to her own house. Ramlal was reluctant, as he knew that his daughter may not receive proper medical attention but Sumitra encouraged her to go back.

On reaching her house, Aruna and her baby were received with singular lack of warmth by her in-laws. No sooner had she settled there that all the household chores like cooking, washing, cleaning were entrusted back to her. Her protests to Jagtap that doctors had advised her not to exert and that they could afford a domestic help were ignored. She had been advised to take Penicillin injection every month and after the injection, she would get severe pain and sometimes fever too but there was little sympathy from the family. Jagtap was angry and upset when she told him that doctor had advised her against getting pregnant and he needed protection before physical relations. His indifference and insinuations left her unhappy and depressed. Amar was the only source of happiness amidst her physical and mental agony. Though her breathlessness was not bad, she would often get palpitations and felt very sick at times.

It was during her next visit to the hospital that the doctor told her not to delay the surgery as her heart was quite enlarged and under strain. When she told this to Jagtap, a new tirade started against her and her family. Her mother-in-law accused her parents of cheating them into this marriage by hiding the facts about her heart disease. Her pleas that she or her parents had no idea about her heart illness fell on deaf ears as fresh abuse was hurled upon her. At times the torture would continue for days as if to drive her out of the house. Aruna felt helplessly alone, as she did not wish to burden her father with her woes. Her father had spent his life's savings on the marriage of his four daughters and then a substantial amount when she was in the hospital. He had some land but that was also mortgaged when her youngest sister got married. He had only a short time before he retired from his job. Her brothers were still not earning. Her going to the parental house would mean extra burden on his small income with herself, her son and her illness! She decided to carry on with medicines as long as possible and postpone her surgery.

She also wanted Amar to be little older.

But her physical condition was deteriorating fast. Once a robust and pretty girl, she was now thin and dark with her face looking pale and puffy. The doctors were advising an early operation. During one of the visits to the hospital, she was asked to see the medico social worker, who could help her in arranging financial help in case financial constraint was coming in way of her surgery. Majority of patients coming to the hospital were poor and got help from many charitable organisations in the city. Aruna was in tears, her husband working as middle level officer in government, and she had to go begging to the strangers! She would need around fifty thousand rupees, essentially towards the cost of the disposable equipment used during the operation, as the hospital services were free. She knew that this operation at a private hospital would cost 2 to 3 Lac of rupees. Ramlal tried to cheer up his daughter. He told her that since he was getting retired, he could take care of making rounds of various charities like many others shunting between the hospital and offices of various Trusts. It was humiliating how minions in some charitable institutions treated the needy beneficiaries and kept asking for additional documents. This caused lot of inconvenience and expense to many patients from outside Mumbai.

Aruna empathised with other patients who like her thronged the busy corridors of the hospital. Jagtap as a government employee was entitled for getting medical assistance for himself and his family and Aruna was still his family. She decided to confront Jagtap since he himself was not forthcoming. She pleaded with him that he may not care for her but he must think of his son. Amar needed his mother as also his father. She was herself surprised at her courage when she told Jagtap that if he did not apply for the government assistance, she herself would go and meet his section officer for help. Jagtap was taken aback to hear new and confident Aruna; he put in the application along with the cost certificate from the hospital for the medical assistance. The claim for the expenses was passed. By this time, he had realized that heart operation of Aruna was risky enough and she might not survive the operation. This could absolve him of at least some guilt!

Meanwhile her mother-in-law was constantly complaining about her ill health and the miseries she had brought to her only son. She blamed Aruna for denying him any happiness and pleasures as a dutiful wife. Personal abuse to Aruna had long stopped to bother her but every time her parents were targetted, she smarted under her skin. She could do nothing except crying for hours. She adored her father and held him in high esteem. She was sure that he had not known about her illness before she got married; his self-respect and integrity were never in doubt. Aruna herself would not have agreed to get married had she known about the miseries married life would bring her way. So many times thoughts of ending her cowardly and miserable existence crossed her mind but Amar's innocent and lovely face quickly erased any such thought. She wanted to live and love her child.

Aruna started to prepare for her operation; the heart disease along with the constant stress of living through a bad relationship with Jagtap had taken a heavy toll on her health. Her emaciated body however, housed a very alert and sensitive mind that constantly worried about future of her son, Amar, in case she did not survive the operation. More she learnt about the risks of her heart disease and operation, more she wanted to live.

She would fight death, she decided even as she hardened her feelings towards an indifferent Jagtap. She knew her parents were growing old and had had enough share of misfortunes. She made her younger sister tearfully promise her to take care of Amar if Aruna did not make it through the operation. Doctors had told her that the risk of valve replacement surgery as such was quite low but since she was physically very weak, this could result in some complications.

Aruna was admitted to the hospital as scheduled. By this time she knew all about her surgery and also about the post operative care from some small booklets that doctor had given to her while fixing her appointment for surgery. She heard with care what the anaesthetist and the young house surgeon had to tell her. Jagtap came to see her before the operation. After years of loveless togetherness, Aruna was surprised and angry with herself that she still felt affectionate towards him. She told him that she had not been able to make him happy and would make up for all the lost time once she became all right. She was suddenly afraid of the big operation, she told him, and desperately wanted Jagtap to tell her that all would be well between them after her operation but he said little that could comfort Aruna. She did not want to die, at least not as yet! Jagtap's mother who had accompanied him for the first time to the hospital sat there, without saying a word, guessing chances of her survival! Ramlal and her sisters tried to cheer her even as they unsuccessfully tried to hide their own tears.

The night before the operation, Aruna was given a sedative but this only resulted in a sleep mired with nightmares. She was seeing the distorted faces of doctors and nurses, but amongst many unknown faces was one familiar face of Jagtap too! She saw him forcing himself on her as she was left gasping for breath. She screamed as the nurse injected her with first shot of pre-medication and antibiotics and wheeled her towards the hold area in the operation suite.

The ward boy and the nurse pushing the gurney stopped in front of the white doors of the operation suite. Ramlal took Amar close to his mother's emaciated cheeks. Amar could hardly recognise the woman in green gown with her head covered with a green cap as his mother who was going to fight the biggest battle of her life so that she could live for him. Jagtap took hesitant steps towards the stretcher but stopped short. Aruna felt gentle touch on her face as she tried to focus her groggy eyes on her father before they rested on Amar. She gave a weak smile as she pressed Amar's podgy hand and whispered softly, 'don't trouble Aajoba - I will be back soon' - her eyes had closed even before she had completed her sentence.

She was wheeled inside the operation room with its walls lined with light green tiles. There were animated voices amidst clutter of instruments and carefree chat of the nurses as they laid down their instruments and the technicians were setting up their machines. Aruna was transferred from the gurney on to the narrow operation table. She felt the cold hands of nurse fixing the electrodes on her back for recording the EKG. Aruna though sleepy looked around and observed a huge TV screen lit up with bright green and yellow lights and she could hear the loud bleeps of her own irregular heartbeats.

She heard the gentle voice of her surgeon reassuring her and holding her hand as the anaesthetist inserted the first I.V line on the back of her hand. She found Trish's presence reassuring before she was put to sleep under anaesthesia.

A Portex tube had been passed down her trachea and connected to the respirator. A fine plastic tube was introduced in Aruna's left wrist and bright red blood spurted out as the needle hit the radial artery. This tube was connected through a longish plastic tube to the transducer and her arterial blood pressure was being displayed on the monitor along with digital readings of Heart rate and the Blood pressure. The anaesthetist then introduced a catheter with multiple ports into her neck vein so that two or three drips carrying essential drugs could be given simultaneously. One port would be used to measure central venous pressure as well.

The surgical resident had already finished with passing a Foley's catheter in order to keep a close watch on the urine during and after the surgery. Temperature probes were in place to monitor the body temperatures.

The resident proceeded to clean the entire chest and abdomen and applied viscous solution of concentrated iodine, giving a dark brown colour to her skin. Nurse covered Aruna's naked body with heavy surgical drapes leaving only a rectangle exposed in the middle of the chest. The chief resident was already there, scrubbed and gowned. He adjusted the drapes slightly and fixed a sticky, clear plastic sheet on the exposed skin. Meanwhile Trish finished her ten-minute scrub with yellowish, frothy iodine solution on her hands and forearms. As she turned the running tap off with her elbow, she said a silent prayer like she always did and pushed the O.R door open with her back. She gently dried the dripping hands with a towel that the scrub nurse handed to her before putting her arms through a sterile gown stretched open in front by the nurse. She slipped her hands into smooth, pre-powdered latex gloves and looked instinctively at the x-ray screen where Aruna's chest x-ray had been mounted on. She noted the large heart shadow on the x-ray, almost filling the ribcage. For Trish working in the haloed speciality of cardiac surgery and that too as the chief, had not come easily. This had always been thought to be a man's world. She believed that what mattered really was hardwork, dedication, stamina. Compassion and patience were the attributes and could be credited to her being a woman!

Trish moved in measured steps to the right side of the table as the chief resident crossed over to the opposite side. The table height adjusted for her short frame of five feet two inches, she asked for a scalpel and following a nod from the anaesthetist, made a steady cut in the middle of the exposed chest through the sticky plastic drape. The attendant had connected the headlight, which Trish had fixed on her head before she scrubbed; she seemed satisfied as the bright white light focussed exactly in the middle of the incision. She continued to deepen the incision with an electric knife, controlling the current with foot pedal and coagulating small bleeders. As she hooked her finger behind the sternal notch, the nurse handed her the electric saw that would cut through the middle of the sternum. The anaesthetist had temporarily stopped the ventilator to prevent inadvertent opening into one of the pleural cavities. As the sternum split into two neat halves, she applied bone-wax to stop the bleeding from the marrow. Trish never forgot to mention to the residents every time she used the bone wax that a neurosurgeon had discovered it. She was particular that young generation of surgeons remember their debt to the pioneers!

As the split halves of the sternum were further spaced apart with a metal retractor the bleeps on the monitor had become faster and irregular orange flashes were indicating that Aruna's heartbeat had quickened. In the gap opened by the sternal retractor, heart could be seen beating irregularly and restlessly within the glistening and tense pericardial sac. Trish slit open the pericardium and large amount of amber fluid gushed out which was sucked out by the assistant. The pericardial edges were lifted and fixed on to the drapes while the sternal retractor was exchanged for a heavier one. Trish got on to work as soft melody of Santoor filled the air. Trish liked to work with music in the O.R. while operating. The music helped her to concentrate on the job and it masked the small noise in the background.

She looked across the table at Joshi, who signalled that he was ready with the heart lung machine. She jabbed a syringe filled with Heparin into the right atrium and drew some blood back into the syringe, to make sure it was in the right place, before injecting all of it. Heparin is essential to keep the blood liquid and to prevent it from clotting while it passes through the plastic tubes. The bypass pump with an oxygenator and transparent tubings of medical grade plastic was already primed with electrolyte solution. The plastic tubings were spread across the chest and after making sure that there were no air bubbles, these were neatly divided by the first assistant. Trish's hands were now moving instinctively as she placed two prolene sutures on top of aorta in a perfect circle, facing each other and passed these through rubber tubings. A small incision was made within these purse string stitches and a metal tip plastic tube was thrust into the aorta and was held by the rubber tubings in place. It was securely connected to the arterial line and fixed to the drapes. Next two large venous cannulae were passed through the right atrium into the superior and inferior veins and connected to the plastic tubing that would draw blood into the oxygenator, 'On pump', escaped simultaneously from the lips of Trish and Joshi.

Joshi had been on this machine for more than twenty years and had watched the cardiac surgery and cardiac surgeons grow. He had acquired great expertise and was highly respected by everyone. An intense man, he watched his console with yellow and orange numbers in a hawk like manner, almost flirting and caressing the knobs to fine tune the controls.

The dark venous blood was directed into the oxygenator that functioned as a surrogate lung and the oxygenated red blood was flowing back into the aorta through a pump just like the normal heart contraction would do. Irrespective of the surgeon on the operating table, Joshi took his own time in getting the patient on or off the pump. Once satisfied, he started to cool the blood to drop the body temperature to 28 degree centigrade. Anaesthetist had already prepared and hung up chilled electrolyte solution, rich with potassium chloride when Trish placed a straight clamp across the aorta cutting away the coronary arteries that supply the blood to the heart. As the heart quivered, it was silenced by injecting cold potassium rich electrolyte solution through the aortic root. This cooled the heart further while the extra potassium ensured added protection to the heart muscle now starved of oxygen. The surgical field had become absolutely clear and quiet as all muscle activity had ceased. Trish made a neat cut, opening the left atrium and exposed the diseased mitral valve by slipping in a curved retractor, named after Denton Cooley, the famous heart surgeon from Texas. The mitral valve, which is normally thin and pliable, had hardened like a rock. It had shrunken with a slit like opening and since the two halves were not closing well, the valve leaked significantly. "It is hardly possible to repair this type of valves with mixed disease", Trish said to no one in particular. She removed small clots carefully as she carefully cut away the diseased valve. She washed the opened heart chamber thoroughly with cold saline, explaining to the residents, "this is necessary to prevent any debris from running off to the brain, once the clamp on the aorta is released and the heart starts to beat. A permanent stroke can mar a perfect operation".

As she inspected the excised valve, she expressed usual frustration that her team was so familiar with - "Until basic living conditions and health care improve for the poor and every child with streptococcal sore throat is treated with penicillin, we will continue to see rheumatic heart disease in numbers that we do". Trish discarded the diseased valve into a bowl held by the scrub nurse as she took shiny plastic obturators to size the artificial valve she would put in place.

Starr-Edward heart valve, designed by legendry heart surgeon Albert Starr along whith his engineer friend Lowell Edward, was the first successful model of artificial heart valve to be used in mitral position in 1960s and had stood the test of time. The valve had a simple design; there was a small silastic (rubber) ball held inside a three-pronged metal frame with cloth covered sewing ring to put thorough the stitches that fix it in place. The idea had been smartly taken from the glass-stopper in the humble soda bottles! Besides it was also the cheapest heart valve available and was quite popular with Indian heart surgeons treating poor patients. The valve had lower complications than more sophisticated designs.

Trish took her usual 12 sutures, neatly distributing andholdingintothreeparts,puttingthemsystematically through the native annulus and then through the cloth ring of the valve. Once all sutures had been put through, the valve was lowered into the left ventricle and after making sure that the ball was moving freely, the sutures were tied and clipped short. Meanwhile additional dose of cold potassium solution was infused after15 minutes to protect the heart muscle. Taking her eyes briefly off the operating field, Trish, looked around from anaesthetist to the pump technician and scrub nurse, as if to make sure all was under control. She started to close the opening into the left atrium. On cue, the head end of the table was tilted down; the anaesthetist started to squeeze the bag to push all trapped air out through the still open left atrium. Joshi had started re-warming the blood by switching the heater on. A mere glance or a simple gesture ensured perfect communication between the team members making spoken word almost redundant. The needle in the aortic root had been connected to a suction line and Trish allowed the operating field to be submerged in blood as she released the aortic cross clamp. The coronary arteries were once again feeding blood to the heart that started to quiver, first gently and then vigorously. Release of cross clamp had replaced the quietness of the O.R. with a suppressed excitement as all eyes were on the heart. As Trish applied two carbon coated electric paddles sandwiching the heart in between, the defibrillator machine was set on 20 Joules. She pressed the button on the paddles delivering the electric shock, the heart was still for a moment and then a strong regular beat had resumed. The heart that was beating irregularly before the operation was now in perfect regular rhythm. Meanwhile, music had changed to an Abhang by Bhimsen Joshi and the atmosphere had relaxed considerably in the O.R. After observing the action of the heart with satisfaction, Trish asked Joshi to give load to the heart as the anaesthetist started to ventilate the patient. The heart and lungs had now resumed their normal function and there was no difficulty in disconnecting the circulation from the heart lung machine. Trish made sure there was no surgical bleeding. The artificial valve could be heard to be opening and closing well. She proceeded to remove the venous tubes. Anaesthetist started intravenous injection of protamine sulphate to neutralise the heparin given earlier. Once sufficient blood from the oxygenator had been transfused to the patient, cannula from the aorta was removed and the holding sutures were securely tied. Trish looked up at the monitors, satisfied she gestured to the Chief resident to cross over and close the chest. Discarding the gloves, she moved over to the anaesthetist's side to make sure all was well. She discussed with the anaesthetist that since Aruna had remained in and out of cardiac failure, it might be a good idea to support her with a small dose of Dopamine. She moved over to the side of heart lung machine, exchanged pleasantries with Joshi and the scrub nurse and slipped out through the swinging O.R doors.

Chief resident, now in last year of his training, took over the command with confidence that had emerged after spending long and laborious hours in the O.R. He put in the drainage tubes and proceeded to put stainless steel wires through the split halves of the sternum. He made sure that there were was no bleeding site, even as the scrub nurse informed that the swab count was correct and he could close the chest. The wires were crossed over and tightened to fix the sternum securely. He closed the scanty muscle and fat over the sternum and then approximated the skin with absorbable stitch that ran under the skin. The neat suture-less scar pleased his patients and he felt a quiet pride in his skills. He often thought that he would have made an excellent plastic surgeon had he not been enamoured by the glamorous backbreaking cardiovascular training programme! The blood marks on the skin were wiped off as the nurse placed a neat dressing over the incision. The attendant ready with pre-cut lengths of Elastic bandage, applied these to cover the dressing. The drainage tubes had been connected through transparent plastic tubes to the bottles. Nurse made sure that the tubes were not filling with blood before pushing away the instrument trolley. She looked at the wall clock, it was 11.45a.m. Quick lunch and she would have to return and relieve the scrub nurse in the following case.

A trolley from the ICU had already been wheeled in; the anaesthetist and the technician were busy disconnecting the lines from the monitor. Aruna was once again visible as heavy drapes were removed and she was gently transferred on to the stretcher and wheeled across to the intensive care.

As the nurses hooked on the IV lines and connected her to the ventilator and monitors, the chief resident made sure all was working well before asking for Blood gas analysis and a portable chest x-ray. He told his junior resident to get the next case ready, as he himself would hang around for a while before he scrubbed for the next case. The immediate postoperative period was most crucial and any small slip could lead to a major problem. Arterial blood gas sample showed satisfactory results. He finally made sure that there was no excessive blood draining through the chest tubes, checked the orders written by his junior and left Aruna under the charge of ICU nurse.

Meanwhile, Trish was talking with Ramlal who had been waiting outside. She felt a surge of emotion for little Amar who was looking at her in a bemused manner. Dressed in scrub suit, her hair covered with a green surgeon's cap and the mask hanging around her neck, she must have made a curious sight! She smiled at him gently and he responded by pushing his hand forward. Trish took his tiny hand and stroked his hair gently before telling him, "your mama is fine, you can see her after a while"!

Ramlal was called in by the nurse but he stepped back terrified on seeing Aruna with several tubes and lines entangling her thin frame in the bed. Ramlal could hardly differentiate his daughter from other patients around, all of them connected through mesh of tubes and wires to huge machines all around. Things were different, however, the next morning as Aruna had been disconnected from the ventilator and once the tube from her throat was removed, she could talk with Ramlal and Amar in soft whispers, her eyes filled with tears. Behind these tears, there was joy of being alive for the sake of her little son. She gestured Amar to come close to her and patted him affectionately. Her movements were still painful. She did not ask her father about Jagtap.

Aruna recovered without any major problems. She co-operated fully with the physiotherapists and the nurses making her recovery very smooth. Once her blood tests had been stabilised and dosages of drugs regulated, she requested the doctor if she could leave the hospital early as the financial limits of her father had been stretched to the limit with no support in Mumbai . Doctors gave the necessary instructions asking her to come back after two weeks for another blood test. Aruna was tongue tied as she struggled to express her gratitude to the doctors and nurses for giving her a new lease of life.

She was already moving about slowly while she was in the hospital. Once home, her activity had picked up. Though her physical pain was not much, mental trauma was agonising. Jagtap had not come to visit her even once in the hospital after the operation. She later came to know that Jagtap had not waited once he got the news that operation had been successful. She wondered if he was disappointed that she actually survived the operation! Aruna was perplexed as to why no one, her father or her sisters and brothers ever mentioned about Jagtap. Her younger sister, Shalini, had been very fond of Jagtap and she was close to him. Even she was quiet when ever Aruna enquired about Jagtap. She had guessed that there was something serious but decided to wait for her family to tell her the truth. The wait was not too long for Aruna soon learnt that Jagtap was not going to come and fetch her. He along with his mother had visited her father's house while she was in the hospital. They informed the family that Aruna was no longer welcome in their house. Jagtap's mother further insulted and embarrassed them by alleging that their sick daughter with her constant ill health had only brought misery to the family. She had decided to get Jagtap remarried. In a condescending manner, she left after saying that Aruna could keep Amar with her if she so desired. On hearing this Aruna was seething with anger. Her pain this time was sharper than the physical pain of major operation she had undergone. She tried hard not to show her hurt. She reasoned with herself that God had given her the fresh lease of life to fight the big battle of her life. Her mission in life from now onwards would be to continue with her life without the crutches of her hollow marriage.

She also decided that she would not burden her father any more. The constant laughter ringing in their house had been replaced by the shadow of sadness hanging around the lives of Aruna and Amar. She told herself that with her faulty heart valve replaced with a new one, her physical condition can only get better and if she followed the doctors' instructions properly, she would be normal and whole once again, ready to chalk her own future. She started to venture out taking Amar to school and felt good as she walked through the streets filled with nostalgia of the carefree days of her childhood. Aruna remembered the happy times that she and her sisters had spent along with friends. She also thought that her desire to study and become independent was perhaps a premonition of her impending difficulties. Aruna approached the Principal of the only woman's college in the town to enquire if she could take her B. A. examinations as a private candidate. The principal not only agreed to forward her examination forms but also agreed to help her prepare for the examinations. It had been long time since she had said good-bye to the books. Her household responsibilities and then her illness and Amar had all conspired to interrupt her studies. She was however, now determined to have no interruptions and make up for the lost years of her life.

She took the B. A. final examinations with full backing and support of her parents and the college principal. She had prepared well and her studies were punctuated only by the periodic but necessary hospital visits for the blood tests and follow up with the doctors. The doctors familiar with upheaval in her personal life were kind to her; she was never made to wait in the endless queues in the clinics. Amar was fully under the charge of her father. Amar in his own cute ways had brought some cheer back in the household. No one was surprised when Aruna passed her examinations with good grades. Ramlal and his wife were very happy and were proud of their daughter. Aruna got a part time teaching assignment even as she took her admission for M. A. Amar was doing fine in the school. Her being at home was also having a positive ripple effect on her younger brothers. They had found a new companion and an inspiration in their sister. The foursome, Aruna, her two brothers and little Amar had formed an informal study group as they discussed topics of common interest. This helped Aruna to understand the younger generation better that helped her immensely when she started teaching in the college. Aruna was extremely popular with her pupils and the staff. She brought several new ideas making the curriculum interesting for the students. What had endeared her most was her interest in environmental issues. There was a beautiful nursery and a horticulture laboratory all with intense personal efforts of Aruna along with some of her students. The nature trails and picnics devoured all her weekends but the fast pace suited Aruna. She had no time to sit and brood over the unhappy memories of Jagtap. Her students performed well and Aruna was making a name for herself in the teaching circles.

Once her job was confirmed, she was offered the job of Warden. She grabbed this offer without any hesitation. She could now establish her independent house and also be near her students. Her parents too had no difficulty in accepting her moving out like this. Aruna bloomed with ideas. Amar was progressing with his studies very well and had inherited Aruna's qualities of hard work, patience and maturity in good measure. He asked no questions about his father. Amar had had no difficulty in assessing the very small role his father had played even while he was an infant. This used to worry Aruna at times. Every time she tried to broach the subject, Amar would gently change the topic or else go out. After a few unsuccessful attempts at bringing him the reality, Aruna too decided to drop the matter.

Aruna was considered as a natural choice for Principal when the Board of trustees planned to start a new residential school at Panchgani. Aruna was given a spacious house. The salubrious climate of the place suited her frail health. Ramlal had retired from job and proved to be an able help to steer her through the teething problems of the new school. Two years after they moved to Panchgani, her mother expired. Her brothers were already in professional colleges. Aruna was very happy that she could look after her father who had stood by her like a rock.

Meanwhile she learnt that Jagtap had got married again. He had suffered a paralytic stroke a few years back. Strangely she felt no anger towards him although he had not even bothered to divorce her before he got married again. The long years of hard work and single-minded devotion to teaching and Amar had washed away all the bitterness that she had for Jagtap. She, in fact, felt strangely relieved that there was somebody to look after him. Jagtap in his own way had given her the biggest opportunity to realise her potential and for her personality to grow and flourish. She could not have achieved the recognition, respect and love of so many people, had she remained in his shadow merely as a sick and helpless wife.

She continued her work with greater vigour. Her hard work and innovative ideas brought rich rewards for the school that though new was much sought after. Her talent and contributions were further recognised when she was awarded President's medal for Best Teacher. Having started late with her career, Aruna was closing the gap fast.

She particularly enjoyed helping the poor children and arranged for scholarships for the deserving. In addition, her house and her free time were always available to the children from the families living around the school. She gave her love in abundance and received it in double measure. Aruna now felt complete. Ramlal did not have to worry about at least this daughter of his when he passed away peacefully in her house a few years after they had moved to Panchgani.

It had been nearly fifteen years since her heart operation and she was one of the few long-term survivors of valve replacement operations, who came to the hospital regularly. It was natural that she was a favourite patient of her doctors, an example what an educated and committed patient with artificial heart valve could achieve! Each time she visited the hospital, she was deeply moved by the sight of helpless poor patients who still crowded the corridors of the hospital just like she had done many years back. It was during one such emotional meeting with her surgeon that Trish suggested that Aruna could help these poor people by forming a support group for patients who had undergone heart surgery. Aruna could not get a better opportunity to repay her debt to the society. After that day, Jagtap vanished even from her memories.

Amar had driven quietly allowing Aruna to revel in her thoughts. They had reached Pune station and he made his mother comfortable in her coach. Aruna reminded him to take care and telephone his welfare as he bid her a proud though tearful farewell as the train started to move. The next stop of her life's journey was going to be the Mumbai Hospital where she had undergone her heart surgery 18 years ago. She had decided to work as a volunteer at the heart surgery department as this was where she had started the real journey of life, rewired and ready to face the tough challenges that had come her way.

WHEN I ALMOST DIDN'T BECOME A CARDIAC SURGEON....

The conventional heart surgery requires presence of large tubes to divert blood from the right side of the heart to an artificial lung or oxygenator for purifying the blood and the same is then returned into Aorta through a pump to be redistributed to rest of body organs like brain, liver, kidneys and other vital organs. The heart-lung machine thus bypasses the heart (and lungs) while carrying out various surgical procedures inside the heart like repairing or replacement of heart valves or performing corrective operations for various birth defects (Congenital heart defects). Coronary artery bypass surgery in contrast requires all the surgical work to be done on surface of the heart allowing these operations to be carried out on "beating heart", without use of heart-lung machine. However, while working inside the heart, use of heart-lung machine is mandatory to have a quite and blood-less field to repair complex heart defects.

The presence of several tubes in the small heart of infants could make the conventional technique quite cumbersome in the initial days of heart surgery. The technique of profound hypothermia and total circulatory arrest was developed to surmount these problems. It was pioneered and popularized by Cardiac Surgeons from New-Zealand and Australia and revolutionized infant cardiac surgery everywhere. In a nutshell, this involved surface cooling by putting ice bags on the the body after the baby was put to sleep with all vital signs monitored continuously. Once the temperature dropped down to around 32 Degree Centigrade, the chest was opened and the baby connected to the heart lung machine with single tube (cannula) in right heart and another in the aorta. The temperatures were lowered further as the blood circulated through chilled tubes. The heart lung machine then stopped completely once the temperature reached 18 Degree Centigrade.

The heart is then at a total standstill and devoid of any blood inside. This facilitates visualizing the defects clearly and same can then be repaired with precision. Once the repair is over and the incision on the heart chamber is closed, the heart lung machine is started again and body temperatures brought up to normal levels before discontinuing the heart lung machine.

The idea of using the cold temperatures for protection of the heart, brain and other organs during this period of 'no circulation' came to cardiac surgeons by observing the polar beers who burrow deep into snow, for as long as 6 months, without any food or nutrition. This is possible only because the cooling lowers the metabolism of the body significantly reducing the energy requirements of the body. One question that bothered the surgeons was as to "how long the circulation can be stopped without having any adverse effect on the brain"? At normal body temperature of 37° C, the brain has only 3 minutes as safe period and if circulation can not be restarted, it can suffer irreversible damage. That is why external cardiac massage is so very important in cases of cardiac arrest - idea is to reach sufficient blood and oxygen to the brain. But the temperatures are lowered considerably, this period of protection becomes longer. At 18 degree Centigrade, we have up to 30 minutes or even longer to conclude the operation without fearing brain damage with some surgeons extending the safe limits even up to 45 minutes of total circulatory arrest.

I was in the O.R. early as I did not want to miss the chance to scrub for my first pediatric case.

The junior house surgeons those days did not scrub with the chief; in fact most often they did not get to scrub at all as their roles were restricted to arranging operation lists, collecting investigations reports from different laboratories and making frequent trips to the blood bank. So when the chief asked me to scrub with him the next day and that too for a pediatric case, there was flutter in my heart and understandably some heartburn amongst the fellow residents.

Macchindra, 8 months old, was beautiful though a scrawny baby, friendly when he wished to be but cranky most of the time. He had large lustrous eyes with long beautifully curled eyelashes that attracted one instantly towards him! It had been one of the many 'smart' observations that I was busy making those early days of residency that the children with congenital heart disease had beautiful eyes; another one being that most cyanotic (blue) babies were dressed by their mothers in blue, mauve or purple colors! Macchindra's father was one of the employees in the same hospital. He was diagnosed to have a large hole in the heart with elevated pressure in the pulmonary artery that carries blood to the lungs for purification (VSD with severe PH). Mother, Vasanti, reluctant in the beginning to have the heart surgery on her young infant finally agreed to the proddings of an overconfident father. Shantaram though knew nothing about the complexity of operation, his confidence was based upon his working in the hospital and thereby knowing all the senior doctors.

Next morning as I stepped out of the changing room having finished the ward rounds and mandatory visit to the blood bank confirming availability of fresh blood, I saw the Chief entering the lounge. He was early too.

When I entered the OR, Machindra was already anaesthetized. The anesthetist and her juniors were busy placing ice bags strategically on his body and around the head to let the temperature drift by surface cooling. The temperatures were being monitored continuously as were other vital signs. Once the temperatures reached 32 degrees, his chest was opened by a long incision placed in midline. The cardiopulmonary bypass was setup with aortic cannulation and a single venous tube placed in the right atrium. The temperatures dropped further steadily. The heart was looking pale and beating almost leisurely at a much slower rate. It was finally stopped by clamping the aorta while cold potassium cardioplegia solution was injected into the aortic root. The pump was stopped at 18^0 while the venous cannula was removed and the blood was drained into the oxygenator. I had an instant desire to touch and feel the heart which was now cold and still. The right atrium was opened with an incision strategically placed to reveal a large defect in the muscular partition separating the two lower chambers of the heart (ventricular septum). The defect was sutured using a Dacron patch, the incision in the right atrium was closed and the tube was reinserted inside. The circulation had been stopped for only 22 minutes but it seemed like an eternity as I watched the entire drama with a bated breath. Once the circulation was restarted and technician was told to re-warm the patient, my sigh of relief was audible to everyone present there drawing a sharp look from the surgeon! At 37° C, the heart was beating regularly and there was no heart block. As the anesthetist started to ventilate the patient, the heart lung machine was gradually stopped. The operation had gone off in a copy book manner. Macchindra was transferred to the intensive care unit (ICU) and remained stable; he was closely watched and ventilated for forty-eight hours before being weaned off the ventilator. The tracheal tube was removed and by evening most of the lines had also been pulled out. We were basking in the glory of successful operation and waiting to get back at the critics. The euphoria unfortunately was short lived.

Over next few days, first the nurses and then we residents realized that Macchindra could not see. He would smile, make noises and respond playfully but with out focussing his eyes. In next few days the worst fears were confirmed when the eye specialists confirmed that Macchindra was virtually blind! That his beautiful eyes could no longer see upset everybody in the unit but devastated his parents, Shantaram and Vasanti. The tragedy saddened me deeply. I avoided seeing his family even as I made fervent pleas to the neurology and the ophthalmology colleagues to do some thing but they were unanimous that there was virtually no hope of recovery. Macchindra himself was oblivious of the serious handicap; he was playful and charming as he recovered from surgery. His parents initially cursed their fate but slowly the tirade was directed towards the surgical team. The doctors, who were hailed like gods soon after the operation, were instantly turned into villains. We understood their hostility though it still hurt.

After about 3 weeks stay in the postoperative ward, the dilemma facing the unit was what to do next. His family had become quite aggressive and would even get violent at times. His father bluntly told us that he was not going to take a blind child home. The psychiatrists and counselors had already stepped in. The remorse of the doctors was gradually being replaced with a quiet anger brought about predominantly by guilt but also in self-defense. I was torn between my emotional attachment for Macchindra and my loyalty and solidarity with the surgical team. It was finally decided to shift him to the medical ward where chronic patients were usually kept.

The busy schedule of surgical residency continued. I often thought of Macchindra and thought of visiting him in the medical ward but quickly changed my mind one night as an inebriated Shantaram, his father, stood in front of me in abusive and dangerously inimical mood. He was now blaming me directly for his misfortunes. It was I alone who had worked him up for surgery and spent most time in the ward as junior resident. My anger was replaced with guilt when Shantaram broke down and begged for mercy killing of his child. I fumbled for the right responses even as tears were rolling down freely on my cheeks. My medical training had not prepared me to handle situations like this. I felt helpless and must have sounded utterly unconvincing as I repeated the cliche that as a doctor, my job was to give life and not to take it away. I was not sure if Machhindra's life could be called as one. He was not even a year old, and had been deprived of his eyesight, for no fault of his.

That night I gave up my plans of becoming a Cardiac Surgeon.

There was, however, a subtle change in Shantaram after that day's outburst. He came to see me now and then. I had no hopes to share with him though he continued to share his pain with me. He had become very sober after that and I was told that he had given up his drinking. He spent most of his off duty time with Macchindra and was even preparing to take him home. My relations with the parents having healed as they accepted their fate, I would go and see Macchindra whenever possible. Meanwhile, Macchindra's condition had remained an enigma for medical experts. The eye surgeons and the neurologists were not very optimistic about recovery and were flummoxed about the cause of total loss of vision. The possible cause of blindness could have been central artery thrombosis or embolism though this did not explain how both eyes had got affected. A cortical blindness was more likely, but there was no other neurological deficit. As the days passed, we got busy with our routines; there were other successes to celebrate and some failures to mourn about. Macchindra was not forgotten though his tragedy had receded from my mind and the pain was no longer as sharp as it used to be.

One night I had just come back to my room after a grueling day in the O.R. I must have fallen asleep instantaneously but was woken up with the persistent ringing of the telephone outside the room. I was not on call that night, and tried to ignore the bell but it was difficult to go back to sleep with the shrill noise. I reluctantly pulled myself up and reached for the phone. There was an excited voice on the other end, calling me urgently to the medical ward! I screamed into the phone, "I am not on call" but the nurse had already put the phone down on the other side. Having received the call, I was in a fix, what if there is an emergency in medical ward and no CVTS resident showed up?

My eyes were half closed when the lift stopped on the 8th floor. As I neared the medical ward, the excitement on the entire floor was palpable. All lights were on and nurses, ward boys and even the patients were rushing in and out of Ward 17. I looked at my wristwatch; it was 2 a.m. - what was the problem I wondered even as I quickened my pace. Had some patient cut his radial artery or someone had jumped off the 8th floor? Occasionally bizarre cases of attempted suicides used to happen in this ward as most inmates were chronically ill and depressed! As I entered the ward, I saw a very excited Shantaram near the Nursing Station - 'Oh, was he drinking again and had created a ruckus in the ward - I hope he has not harmed Macchindra, 'several thoughts flashed by fast in my mind. He rushed towards me as soon as he saw me and the medical registrar followed him. I stood frozen as there was a mad scramble from all sides. I was not prepared for what I heard next, Shantaram was speaking incoherently, "Doctor, Macchindra can see everything - yes everything and I wanted you to know it first". I was now convinced that he was drinking again as I looked up at the night nurse nervously. The nurse was smiling and nodded her head to confirm what Shantaram had just said. She went on to tell me in a voice choked with emotion, "I went for my usual midnight round. One of the patients was unable to sleep and was asking for a sleeping pill. I wanted to check with the doctor so I returned to the phone. Meanwhile I had left my night reports and pen etc. on the nearby bed. When I came back after telephoning the doctor, my report was not where I had left it. I started looking for my papers and then I saw Macchindra sitting up in his bed. My red ink pen was in his hand and he was merrily drawing lines on my report card! I woke up his mother who was fast asleep; she apologetically took the paper and the pen away from her son without realising that he was drawing. She realized that her son could see only when he put his hand forward and tried to take the paper back from her even as extending his other hand towards the pen. Both of us could not believe what we were witnessing and were in a trance while Macchindra was howling to get the paper and pen back". This had woken up other patients and the other ward staff. The news spread to the other wards on the floor and everybody scrambled to Ward 17 to see the miracle first hand. A fellow ward boy had informed Shantaram who was at home and he came rushing to the hospital. Macchindra meanwhile looked as if nothing had happened and was trying to figure out what was all the fuss about! It had been exactly 3 months (12 weeks), since the fateful day when he was operated upon.

By next morning, there was only one story doing the rounds in the entire hospital. Macchindra had regained his vision unexpectedly just as he had lost it. If there were no explanations earlier, none were forthcoming now. But there was cheer and happiness all around. He had become quite a celebrity, as everyone wanted to see the miracle boy. He was surrounded with gifts and presents from the nurses, doctors, patients, and others. There was a big celebration in our department when Macchindra finally went home.

Macchindra quite unwittingly had also made the big decision for me; ***I did become a heart surgeon.***

KEEPING THE FAITH

Sujatha and Venkat lived in a two-room apartment along with Venkat's parents. Theirs had been an arranged marriage and after the initial hiccups, Sujatha was getting along fine with her in-laws. Venkat's father, Subhiram, had worked in a government office and had lived in Bombay (now Mumbai) all his working life. Venkat was the youngest amongst his three children and only one living with him and his wife, Binduma. His older son, also employed in a bank, was living in Madras (now Chennai) with his wife and two children. The daughter was married to a computer engineer and was living in Canada. After Subhiram retired from service, Binduma had briefly flirted with the idea of settling down in Madras but finally opted to live in Bombay. The choice was actually made by his wife; she thought Bombay was more cosmopolitan and modern where she could have the flavours of tradional South India without shackles of living with orthodox and demanding relatives back home. Matunga, where they lived, was the little south of Bombay. Truckloads of jasmine flowers were flown daily for pujas, weddings and other occasions. Ladies in their Kanjeevaram saris and sparkling diamond nose rings jostled for space in the vegetable market. They celebrated Pongal and Onam with oil baths and traditional 'diyas' as the melodious voice of Subbalakshmi filled the air.

Sujatha and Venkat were both employed in a nationalised bank. Sujatha was a small town girl from Andhra Pradesh and had visited even Hyderabad only once before she found herself in the humdrum of Bombay. Sujatha learnt early that her daily routine would comprise of rushing between the local trains, juggling from office to shopping, and cooking and caring for the family. She was conscious that it would require a fine balance of skills to manage all of these if there was to be harmony in the family. She worked hard to adapt herself to fast paced life and soon was competing with those born and brought up in Bombay. She got up early to finish the cooking, packed tiffin for herself and Venkat before rushing to catch 9.02 fast train to Churchgate; it was either a brisk walk or a shared taxi to reach her bank at Flora fountain. Same routine followed while returning home except often she would finish the shopping for next day. Once she reached home, she would relax over hot coffee and a little 'gupshup' with her mother-in-law before she got busy with cooking. She was a good cook and invariably turned some delicious traditional meals, which her in-laws adored. While she remained busy with the household chores, Venkat shared the family news, investments and local politics with his parents.

Once they were comfortably settled, Sujatha and Venkat had no reason to postpone having a baby. She could work as long as she could and in any case bank jobs were liberal with leave; she could take long leave to look after the baby. Binduma would be delighted to look after the grandchild once she resumed work. Sujatha did not like the idea of calling her mother as she was so orthodox and superstitious compared to her mother-in-law and Sujatha was sure that she would impose many more restrictions on her pregnant daughter. Sujatha's pregnancy continued, Binduma was the most excited person in the household.

Sujatha kept well but as she became rather expansive, it was becoming difficult for her to get in and out of the trains. Sujatha wanted to get over with it fast. So it was with some sense of relief when one night, Sujatha woke up Binduma while she packed her bag to go to the hospital. Sujatha delivered the baby normally within hours of reaching the hospital. She only had to look at Binduma's face to intuitively know that it was a boy!

Venkat brought Sujatha and baby home after four days and with traditional rituals, the boy was named Srinivas.

Srinivas was a fine baby but Sujatha could not quite understand as to why he was so irritable especially whenever she was feeding him. He would howl with hunger but no sooner she started feeding him, he would get restless and seemed troubled. Before he was a month old, little Srinivas was looking sick. He was not only having difficulty in feeding but he was breathing very fast and she could see his chest heaving in an ominous manner. She put her hand on his forehead; it felt very hot and was covered with beads of perspiration. She phoned Venkat as she herself rushed to call the family doctor. Dr.Suryavanshi had been the family physician since Venkat was a child and the family had great faith in his opinion. He examined the child and gave him some syrup to bring down the fever. He advised that they see the specialist, Dr. Mehta and the appointment was fixed for the same evening. By evening baby's condition had stabilised, he had even managed a small feed but was still running fever as they prepared to take Srinivas for Dr. Mehta's opinion.

Sujatha missed a couple of heartbeats on reaching Dr. Mehta's clinic as she scanned the doctor's nameplate that read Dr. Mehta as a Cardiologist, specialising in the heart diseases of children. "Why would Dr. Suryavanshi refer Srinivas to Dr. Mehta", she asked Binduma nervously.

Dr. Mehta examined the baby carefully before advising her that baby would need to be admitted in the hospital immediately as he was suffering from pneumonia. He promptly handed over a slip for admission to the children's hospital.

Sujatha's face had turned a shade paler and her heart was beating real fast. Dr. Mehta made her and Binduma understand that he suspected that baby had a hole in the heart but he could confirm it only after the baby's condition had stabilized and some more tests had been carried out. Sujatha got Srinivas admitted in the hospital and waited for Venkat's arrival. Both of them sat by the side of Srinivas who had an oxygen mask put on the face and the nurse had given some injections as prescribed by Dr. Mehta. Binduma was trying to calm down Sujatha though her own anxiety and worry were written large on her face. She was suddenly looking older by several years. Subhiram, who had generally kept himself aloof from the family responsibilities limiting his interactions to the bare essentials, felt the need to take charge first time since he had retired. He decided not to let the things slip as many relatives and friends were dropping by with as many suggestions and opinions.

Srinivas showed significant improvement within days with the antibiotics and other medications and was allowed to be brought home. He was looking better and took the feeds without much problem. He even managed an occasional smile. Dr. Mehta had advised some x-rays and other tests. Sujatha took leave from the office and took the baby for the tests, all the time praying fervently that all would be normal. Dr. Desai, who was doing the echocardiography for the baby made Sujatha sit with the baby and showed her the beating heart of Srinivas as he moved a tiny box on the naked chest of Srinivas, who was fast asleep with the syrup given to quieten him. Sujatha was sitting there dazed and understood nothing as the doctor was pointing out to her pictures of the tiny heart on the screen. She could only make out that the bright blob on the screen was moving and that was the beating heart of her precious baby. She was desperately trying to control her own heartbeat, afraid it might confuse the doctor testing her baby's heart. Dr. Desai interrupted her pensive silence as he pointed some images on the screen and said "There are two large holes in his heart and as a result the pressure in the pulmonary artery (blood line to the lungs) is very high that we call as pulmonary hypertension". He turned his face away from the machine as he made some drawings on a paper, explaining simultaneously, "normally right chambers of the heart are separated from the left by a complete partition. In his case, both partitions, in the upper and lower chambers, are incomplete resulting in two large defects and that is why, pulmonary hypertension has grown so fast".

Sujatha could not believe or understand as why on earth her child's heart should have any defects; she felt weak at the knees and passed out in the arms of her husband, stoically standing next to her.

That very moment, their lives had changed forever.

Thoughts of the baby with heart disease were not the only ones that were going to worry them; there were added feelings of guilt, doubts and tremendous pain. Several doubts were going through their minds. If Sujatha thought this as a retribution for past Karma, Venkat felt guilty that Sujatha had to work almost till term. Could this be because they were not careful enough or was it some infection caught in the crowded trains or was it some curse; Venkat felt perhaps he should have insisted on sending her to her mother's place, that way she would have got proper rest that he was unable to provide. Many irrelevant thoughts tormented both of them at the same time but they, who used to share all their feelings since they had got married, had turned silent. Communicating with each other had never been so difficult.

Binduma meanwhile was doing rounds of all her favourite temples. She made quick pilgrimages to Tirupati and Puttaparthy praying for some divine intervention.

However the ground realities were different. Srinivas had not gained much weight and in spite of the medicines, continued to get frequent respiratory infections requiring antibiotics. He remained irritable most of the time and Sujatha's patience was running out.

Over next three to four months, he had had put on only a few grams in weight and being a tall baby, was looking very lean and emaciated.

Sujatha had extended her leave while Venkat had started to put in overtime. In between, visits to the different doctors continued. Doctor Mehta had recommended an open heart operation at the earliest as it was most unlikely that the large holes in his heart would close on their own. In addition, due to increased flow of blood through the lungs, he remained prone to get frequent chest infections and even another bout of pneumonia. An early operation was the only chance for the baby though the operation itself was highly risky. He had also warned them, "Srinivas's best chance is only if you can manage to take him to London or USA since there are not many centres in India that specialize in open heart surgery in such small babies. Of course, it will cost lot of money but I must tell you the facts as they are". Sujatha and Venkat heard the doctor in silence. They, like any other parents, wanted the best medical care for their baby but did not know how to go about to get him operated upon even in India. Also there was no guarantee that the operation would be successful even if, somehow, they could manage to go abroad.

While they waited, the baby had lost further weight and was so weak that he could hardly turn on his own. Only his bright eyes looked even larger on his tiny frame. The entire family was watching this downhill course with great anguish and pain. Srinivas was falling behind in development as Sujatha found out when she compared notes with neighbors and friends, babies turning by the age of 3 months; sitting with support by 5 to 6 months and crawling, walking by 10 months of age. Why her sister's son had started to walk by the time he was 9 months of age!

Their personal lives had been completely shattered. Sujatha and her husband had not exchanged single pleasantry since the day Srinivas was diagnosed to have heart disease. They avoided looking at each other, each of them engulfed by a very private sense of guilt and sorrow. May be they just felt inadequate to give hope or support to each other. Their communications were solely restricted around Srinivas's health, medicines, visits to the doctors and the mounting expenses. They barely ate and slept just enough to survive and regain strength to start looking for answers from different people. All the waking hours were occupied finding out what they could do to get Srinivas alright. This took precedence over everything else. They gathered as much information about the disease, the operation, the doctors and the hospitals as possible. Some doctors they had consulted advised a staged operation while the others told them that the operation could be carried out at one time itself. Risk of operation was very high because of severe pulmonary hypertension but if the baby survived the initial period, he had a good chance. They could not understand all of the technical jargon but were intelligent enough to understand the gravity and seriousness of the situation. Binduma's pujas and fasts were bearing no results and pragmatic as she was, she convinced Subhiram to sell their village house to raise some more funds. She bravely prepared her son and daughter-in law for the operation.

Sujatha's fears worsened as Srinivas required another hospitalisation for what the doctor called heart failure. On this occasion, the pediatrician tersely told them that he could no longer continue to treat a surgical condition with medicines alone. He handed them a letter of reference to the Cardiac Surgeon in a local hospital. Sujatha's own health was dipping low on account of constant stress and anxiety about Srinivas but this was no time to worry about herself.

Once the date of operation was fixed, the trips to temples and priests also increased. Subhiram was the most composed and confident amongst all the family members. He decided that the operation would be done at Bombay only although his elder son wanted them to come to Madras as he had seen reports of successful heart operations on children at a local railway hospital.

Srinivas was admitted in the hospital few days before Diwali. When the hospital doctors explained to the family all the details related to Srinivas's disease and operation, they heard with rapt attention hanging on to every syllable and nuance although they had been hearing all this for last 10 months. On the day of operation, Sujatha held her son in her arms as he slept after the premedication. She watched with a heavy heart as Srinivas was taken to the operation theatre. She suddenly felt so empty as Srinivas was not there for her to fill her arms even as she hoped that the emptiness was only temporary. Not only Sujatha, Venkat also felt vacant and numb; they held on to each other for a few moments and then prayed silently as the operation progressed inside. That there were other people in the waiting room besides them went unnoticed.

Once inside the O.R, Srinivas was hooked on to a monitor screen where his ECG and temperatures were being displayed. Srinivas though nearing 10 months of age weighed a miserable 5.8 Kg and was a challenge for the anesthesiologist to insert fine catheters that would monitor his heart beat, blood pressure and oxygenation levels continuously during and after the surgery.

Trish was getting ready for the surgery as she scrubbed vigorously her forearms and hands with medicated soap. She looked at the thin limbs of her little patient, sprawled on the operation table that seemed excessively large for his size. The nurse helped her to don the gown and the gloves as she moved towards the table. The resident doctor who was going to be the first assistant in the operation had already cleaned and draped the baby appropriately. After getting the signal from the anesthetist, Trish cut through the middle of the chest painted brown with iodine. As she divided the breastbone with the heavy scissors, Sujatha's face flashed past before her eyes. Trish had briefly stopped over in the waiting room to talk with her and Venkat on way to the operation theatre. She had noticed how distraught both of them were.

Srinivas was deftly connected to the heart lung machine cannulating aorta and both the major veins connected to the right heart. Once the appropriate flow was established, cooling was started as the plastic tubes carrying the blood passed through the cooling chamber of the heart lung machine chilled with plenty of ice. The heart-lung machine had taken over the function of both these organs. The heart, now empty of all blood, was apparently relieved of pushing large amount of shunted blood and was free from the strain. The heart rate dropped a little as the cooling progressed. At 25 degree Centigrade, the heart was stopped by clamping the aorta even as cold electrolyte solution enriched with potassium was injected into the aortic root.

The interior of the heart was exposed by a neatly placed incision in the upper chamber of the heart (right atrium). A large defect was seen in the upper chamber and a suction catheter was slipped across it. As the blood cleared, the right sided heart valve (tricuspid valve) was lifted with delicate hooks bringing another big defect underneath the tricuspid valve to view.

Nurse handed Trish a sterile pack of the Dacron patch. A large piece was fashioned and cut using a fresh pair of scissors. The large VSD (lower and the bigger of the two defects) was closed first with special sutures to sew the patch of Dacron covering the defect completely and securely. Trish explained the finer details of the operation to the young, enthusiastic students training to become heart surgeons as she continued to take delicate stitches and pointed out with a gleaming forceps, "this is the area where the conduction tissue is at risk and if stitches damage this area, the child can end up having a permanent heart block. Temporary pacemaker wires will be fixed in all such cases". The first assistant was still bleary eyed from the long night that he had to spend in the O R for an emergency valve replacement. He though tried to look attentive and peered over to have a look inside the tiny heart. After closing the VSD and satisfied with the placement of stitches, Trish proceeded to close the second defect in the upper chamber. That was done with greater ease. She looked over the assistant's shoulders towards Mr. Joshi, the technician running the heart-lung machine, signaling him to start warming the patient. Joshi switched from cooling to heating mode of the heat exchanger in the circuit to re-warm the patient. The operation meanwhile progressed smoothly. The clamp across the aorta had been removed and the air was carefully removed by gently massaging the heart with hand and then using suction on the needle inserted in the top of aorta. Trish smiled behind her mask and her eyes twinkled as the heart started to beat slowly and intermittently to begin with but soon picked up more regular and vigorous beat. If it had not been so, she would have to give an electric shock to the heart with tiny paddles already fixed on the surgical drapes and connected to the defibrillator machine. As the temperatures were nearing normal, the heart was beating in regular and rhythmic beats. Trish was relieved that there was no heart block. She fixed tiny pacemaker wires on the surface of the heart as a precautionary measure. The anesthetist had started squeezing the bag to ventilate the patient, in anticipation of disconnecting the baby from the heart lung machine. She checked all the intra-venous drips, zeroed the pressure lines afresh and made sure the infusion rates of dopamine and nitro-glycerine being administered to the baby were in correct doses precisely calculated for the body weight. With a final confirmation from the anesthetist, the heart lung machine was slowly cut off and finally stopped as the heart started taking the load, almost like resuming the duty after a brief holiday. The heart was now looking robust and was beating vigorously, maintaining good blood pressure and venous pressures as displayed continuously on the monitor. The tension in the O.R was suddenly eased, there was an increase in the activity in the O.R and whispers changed into a flurry of voices. Trish removed the tubes and catheters from the heart in a sequence, carefully tying the sutures that had hitherto held these tubes in place. The Protamine Sulphate was given intravenously to help the blood to clot. Two plastic tubes were passed through fresh cuts made in the skin, a little distance from the earlier cut in the middle of the chest. These tubes would drain any blood that may collect around the heart during the post-operative period. The nurse checked to make sure the correct count of swabs and instruments used during the operation, before the heavy Ethibond sutures were put through the two split halves of the breastbone and securely tightened. The assistant crossed over to close the chest as Trish removed her gloves; she was satisfied and happy that all had gone well and yet apprehensive and planning about post operative recovery that could possibly be stormy. She knew that the pulmonary pressure was very high before the surgery and this could cause difficulties ahead. She decided to continue with the medications to lower the pulmonary pressure as also to keep Srinivas on the ventilator for next 48 hours. This would allow the heart and lung functions to recover and stabilize. She came out into the waiting area to inform the parents that so far the things had gone well with Srinivas.

Sujatha and Venkat were sitting in the hard plastic chairs almost transfixed and oblivious as to how many hours they had been in the same position since their child had been taken inside the operation room. They had been praying continuously but silently while Binduma was not taking any chances and had been chanting names of all the gods that she could remember. Sujatha and Venkat looked anxiously at the doctor who gently put her hand on Sujatha's shoulder. They had noticed the glint in the doctor's eyes and sensed all was OK even before Trish spoke to them. Sujatha started sobbing incessantly and thanking everyone present there. She was incoherent in her hour of new-found happiness and bliss. Trish was happy to tell the ecstatic parents that she too was happy the way the operation had gone so far and gently warned them of an equally difficult period ahead in the ICU. It was only after the baby was taken off the ventilator successfully and was able to maintain satisfactory blood pressure and oxygen levels effectively on his own that the operation could be called successful. They both felt quite inadequate to express their gratitude to the doctor who had shown tremendous courage to accept the challenge to operate despite the high risk.

Same evening, the nurse took Sujatha and Venkat inside the ICU to see Srinivas. The intensive care unit was very intimidating as they cautiously followed the nurse towards the bed where Srinivas was recovering from the operation. There were huge machines all around even as the nurses rushed from one bed to the other. Sujatha was conscious that there were other patients in the ICU and her eyes were looking for only one bed- where her Srinivas was battling for his life. Tiny baby was hardly visible within the mesh of wires and tubes; he was deeply sedated and a machine was breathing for him. Sujatha was horrified to see the red blood trickling through the transparent plastic tubes coming out of his pale chest which itself was covered with pinkish elastic bandage. The resident doctor on duty reassured them by pointing out to stable heart beat and blood pressure tracings on the monitor. Sujatha bent down and gently touched the exposed hand of her baby, transferring loads of energy laced with love and blessings to Srinivas in that brief touch even as she herself felt completely drained. She looked at Venkat as if to confirm whether Srinivas had actually smiled at her. Escorted outside in the waiting room, Sujatha suddenly felt exhausted and as the fatigue of past nine months took over her body, she felt asleep. Binduma meantime had successfully converted the corner of the waiting room into a personal temple. She had already developed strong bonds with the relatives of other patients. They shared each other's anxieties, grief, and ecstasy as they prayed collectively.

Sometime during the night, Venkat was woken up by the increased activity inside the ICU with nurses and doctors scurrying past through the half-opened doors. He could hear the heavy equipment being rolled in - was Srinivas having some complications, he worried as he looked enquiringly at the doctors passing in and out but they had no time to stop and tell him anything. Venkat looked at Sujatha, huddled into deep slumber on the couch. He had realised long back that he had been totally outclassed by her tenacity and courage in the last nine months. But now when she slept there, he noticed the lines of fatigue and how the stress had taken a toll on his wife. She seemed to have aged in past few months. He decided not to wake her up and tried engaging a ward boy into conversation. He told Venkat that another patient, Peter Fernandez, who was recovering after a valve replacement surgery in the ward, had to be brought back to the ICU as he suffered a sudden cardiac arrest in the ward. The doctors had tried to revive the heart with cardiac massage and electric shocks. Fortunately, the heart had started beating again and Peter was brought to the ICU where he had been connected to ventilator and other life support machines. As Venkat returned to his seat filled with relief, he saw Peter Fernandez's wife entering the ICU; her eyes red and swollen. She was crying and telling that she had gone home only after Peter had had his dinner and he was looking so fine. He suffered a sudden cardiac arrest some time after that. Her son had rushed to bring her to the hospital afraid that Peter might not be even alive when they reached the hospital. Doctor was in the doorway, groggy having worked through the night as he gave a quick summary of events to Peter's wife and about Peter's serious condition even though they had been able to start his heart. As Peter's wife and son sat down in chairs nearby, Venkat went and put his hand on the shoulder of the young man who gave him a grateful look. Venkat's thoughts turned to the young doctors too. By now Venkat was used to seeing them at all odd hours either in the O.R or ICU and when not there, they were with the patients in the wards, writing notes, changing dressings or drawing blood for laboratory tests! He was wondering, when do these doctors sleep or for that matter eat? He was at the same time annoyed but only momentarily as he thought that this doctor could have stopped and reassured him that Srinivas was O. K. or least given him a smile of reassurance but no he was there only to brief Peter Fernandez's wife, no more! He tried telling himself that though these young men were certainly not the best of the communicators yet they were a wonderful lot. Coming from far off places away from the comforts of home, they slogged for long hours inside and out of operation theater for patients and to learn the art and science of cardiac surgery hard way. It was past three in the morning when Venkat closed his eyes even as Sujatha was stirring to get up! She opened her eyes and abruptly sat up, she had just seen Srinivas in her dream and he was calling out to her. Almost next instance, she heard announcement-calling relatives of Srinivas! Venkat and Sujatha nearly jumped to rush towards the ICU and were told that Srinivas had had two episodes of what is called 'pulmonary hypertensive crisis' but had been managed with the medications! Sujatha felt guilty that she had dozed off when she should have continued with her prayers. She inquired from the doctor if he had informed the senior doctor about Srinivas's progress and if everything was being done as per her instructions. The resident doctor reassured her that these episodes were not quite unexpected and they had kept the baby on appropriate medications to tide over the crisis. They had also kept the baby sedated to avoid any stress like pain, noise and anxiety.

Trish herself was there before the clock struck five. Trish liked the silence of early morning hours in the hospital. She was fascinated to see the night duty nurses finishing their chores like sponging and cleaning before they got busy to fill in the night reports. There was a sense of anticipation of new beginning as the dark night ended heralding the dawn. It brought a new hope for some patients and their relatives as one difficult night came to an end. There was no rush of the morning hours, no crowds with the accompanying noise. There was an unsaid but definite tension felt through the day as the overworked staff tried to cope with the demands of equally stressed patients. This somehow melted away as the night tamed the arrogance bringing out more humane side of health workers. The hospital almost seemed inviting and hospitable ready to welcome the chaos of another day.

Today also as Trish entered the empty corridors of the hospital, she walked slowly and softly through the calm and nearly silent floor towards the ICU pausing only for a few seconds to look at the relatives huddled in whatever space they could manage to snatch a little rest.

She was greeted by a couple of resident doctors who were rushing to their rooms for a short nap followed by a quick bath and a hurried breakfast. Of course they might spend a little time over the dining table to gossip about how they had to sort out the mess created by the bosses! They would then rush back to the wards or the O.R to start another day. They were expected to be alert and fresh like they were just returning from a rejuvenating holiday! Trish greeted Dr. Swami, a senior registrar in cardiology, his shoulders almost drooping with the burden that he always seemed to carry on his scrawny frame. He somehow believed that something would definitely go wrong moment he stepped out of the ICCU! Trish made way to the surgical ICU and walked straight to Srinivas as the resident gave her short resume of the events during the night, she seemed to be pleased with his progress.

By next evening Srinivas had been taken off the ventilator though he was still connected to lot of monitors, IV lines and tubes. Sujatha and Venkat were escorted to his bedside and this time they made their way more confidently. Srinivas looked to be in deep sleep, his face peaceful and he was breathing quietly so different from the way he used to breathe early or so Sujatha thought. The nurse encouraged both of them to come close and touch the baby, talk to him. Sujatha's touch was light like a wisp of cotton, afraid to hurt her baby but Srinivas instantly opened his eyes almost sensing her presence. A faint smile on the lips and sparkle of recognition in the eyes were soon replaced with a full throated cry. Sujatha and Venkat, both frightened, looked at the nurse, who signaled them to leave the ICU even as she gave some more sedation to Srinivas.

Srinivas progressed well, doctors were as happy as was the family. Soon he was the favourite patient of nurses and the other attending staff. Once back in the general ward, his recovery was unexpectedly quick. He was chirpy and cheerful with a good measure of tantrums thrown in between especially whenever Sujatha was around. They were finally told that they could take him home. For Sujatha it was an exhilarating experience though the thoughts of taking care of Srinivas after heart surgery were intimidating.

First few weeks at home were difficult as Sujatha tried to translate difficult hospital regimen at home. But she gave that up soon as Srinivas recuperated fast. By end of first month, his appetite was voracious and he had also gained some weight. He was now looking healthier than ever before and Sujatha was encouraged to return to her job as Binduma showed confidence to take care of Srinivas. All was going well, by another six months he was standing up and it was not very late after that when he started walking too. For Sujatha and rest of the family the day he took his first step was a momentous one with happy tidings as he was nearly two and half years of age. He faltered once while he took his first step but got up again and there was no stopping after that. Binduma had to often plead with him that her old knees were not in a position to chase him. Subhiram was back to his old lazy ways, ensconced in easy chair with his trademark newspaper in hand though he glanced happily every now and then towards happy bonding between the grandmother and the grandson.

As the routine of the family returned to normal, Binduma wanted to go to Tirupati and Puttaparthy as she had vowed before Srinivas was operated upon. She persuaded her husband to take Srinivas with them. This was first time Sujatha and Venkat were alone and together after Srinivas was born 3 years ago. They felt almost uncomfortable to be together without talking about illness and treatment of Srinivas. They had hardly exchanged any pleasant thought with each other during these three years; each feeling guilty and responsible for bringing so much unhappiness to the other. Now that all was fine once again, they were at a loss as where to begin. Sujatha fell into Venkat's arms and both of them were crying their hearts out. They felt light and cleansed after this emotional catharsis. They were convinced that it was the blessings of Sri Sathya Saibaba alone that Srinivas had been blessed with successful operation. As token of their gratitude, when Srinivas returned with grandparents after propitiating all gods, Sai was added as a prefix to his name and he became Sai-Srinivas!

All was going well for them now, except that Srinivas still had not started to talk. Visits to the pediatricians and the neurologists revealed no abnormality. He was seen by the speech therapists but they too found nothing wrong with him. Sujatha was worried but did not quite know what to do. He was nearly four years old. He was naughty like other children and played whole day even as Sujatha and Binduma pleaded with him not to run around too much.

The family planned to go to Puttaparthi during Puja holidays for Sai Darshan and to celebrate Srinivas's fourth birthday. It had not been easy for them to take time off together especially when she had been away from work for so long. The entire family was excited to go together on this pilgrimage. They reached Bangalore by train and from there boarded a bus to reach Puttaparthy. There were devotees from all over the country in the bus and Sujatha found it a very peaceful and happy experience. As the bus wound its way towards Puttaparthy, they were transported to a different world. There were fields on both sides of the road interspersed with small kiosks and shops decorated with pictures and posters of Sathya Saibaba. The devotees became very excited as they neared the destination; they were singing Bhajans and thanking the lord for this blessed opportunity.

Sujatha and Binduma too were singing bhajans filled with joy and bliss till Sujatha stopped abruptly in the middle of the rendering of a bhajan. Her expression almost of shock and eyes wide open with surprise as she watched Srinivas too was singing with them! The shock and surprise were soon replaced with an ecstasy hitherto unknown to her. The doctors and the speech therapists had not been able to make him utter even a syllable and here he was singing loudly and clearly. Venkat, his parents and Sujatha were all in a state of bliss and nobody cared to wipe the tears flowing freely and washing their faces! The other pilgrims too felt blessed to witness this miracle. They spent a happy week at Puttaparthi going for Darshan and Bhajans every morning and evening.

Sujatha, back in Bombay, was hesitant to narrate the incidence to anybody, as nobody would believe her. Sai Srinivas was enrolled in the school and has progressed well.

Sai Srinivas is a 24 years old young man doing Masters in an Engineering College in Mumbai. For the Srinivas family, it is only a matter of faith.